Faithful and Fair

Faithful and Fair

Transcending Sexist Language in Worship

Keith Watkins

Abingdon
Nashville

FAITHFUL AND FAIR:
TRANSCENDING SEXIST LANGUAGE IN WORSHIP

Library of Congress Cataloging in Publication Data

WATKINS, KEITH.
    Faithful and fair.
    Includes bibliographical references.
    1. Sexism in liturgical language. I. Title.
    BV178.W37   264   80-39698
            ISBN 0-687-12707-6 (pbk.)

MANUFACTURED BY THE PARTHENON PRESS AT
NASHVILLE, TENNESSEE, UNITED STATES OF AMERICA

In grateful appreciation
To three generations of the family who have taught me so much
of justice and truth:

Lydia Hiukka Watkins—Harold S. Watkins
Ellen Lefebre Caton—Edgar F. Caton

Billie

Sharon, Marilyn,
Michael and Diane
Carolyn, Kenneth

*To the many persons whose faith and practice have influenced
the shape of this book on liturgical reform, and especially:*
The Christian Church in Manilla, Indiana,
in whose Sunday service
these prayers first were offered to God
The School for Congregational Leaders, Des Moines, 1979
Members of Bicycle Pilgrimages in 1979 and 1980
Disciple Consultation on Worship, 1980
Commission on Faith and Order (NCCC),
Consultation on Baptism, Eucharist, and Ministry, 1980
Colleagues at Christian Theological Seminary
Marjorie Sharp

CONTENTS

Everliving God, may your Name be praised!
Before the worlds began, you were; and when this
created order disappears, you will continue to be . . .
  Majesty and Beauty
  Justice and Truth,
  Power and Mercy.
Because of the boundlessness of your love,
you opened your womb,
  pouring forth your own inner life,
  giving birth to the world, and
  bestowing on it life like your own.
Moment by moment your Spirit continues to surge
through all that is, continually renewing the creative act
with which it all began.

All of which we remember today,
  when the sun is becoming warm again,
  when the flowers show their color, and
  when the hope of spring is upon us.
On this day especially do we praise you because we here celebrate
your mighty act that restored life to Jesus who had been put to
death by evil men and women.
  Like the disciples, we can scarcely believe the report;
  yet your own living power within us confirms
  the truth of the ancient Easter story.
Everliving God, may your Name be praised.

The Challenge
to Conventional Language

1

And I heard the altar cry,
"Yes, Lord God, sovereign over all,
true and just are thy judgements!" (Rev. 16:7 NEB)

The language of worship, until now heavy with the metaphors of masculinity, is changing. Even if we wanted to stop the process, there is no power strong enough to keep these changes from coming to pass, for this movement at the very center of the church's life is impelled by energies that are gaining strength—energies generated by renewed Bible study, reassessments of human experience, the reconstruction of theology, and the reordering of the church's structures. We do not yet know how to pray as we ought. All that now is clear is that the time is coming when the language of worship will express the nature of God more truly and of humanity more justly than does the vocabulary of prayer commonly used today.

This new movement has taken many people by surprise. During the past thirty-five years we have experienced dramatic changes in the language of the sanctuary. Most American Christians have exchanged their King James or Douay Bibles for one of the modern speech translations or paraphrases. The archaic, reverential use of *thee* and *thou* has dropped out of most public prayers, and most of us can no longer wrap our tongues around the *eth* and *edst* with which some verbs used to end. The way we talk in worship is simpler than it used to be. All these changes are so much a part of current worship experiences that we are scarcely aware of them.

Just as we are settling down to the full enjoyment of this new, brisk, and contemporary language of prayer, the new challenge has crashed upon us, one that confuses and unsettles us more than have any of these other changes. This new challenge questions the language of Scripture, of hymns, and traditional prayers, of instructions in worship books and the ways we talk in conversation. Critics of traditional liturgical language are showing how the conventional language of prayer is based on a falsely dualistic understanding of reality, how many of its portrayals of God are misshapen and idolatrous, and how it consistently states an anthropology that distorts the true nature of both women and men.[1]

What is at stake now is more than felicity of language. It is truth and justice. The very nature of God and the character of religious experience are involved in this debate over the use of exclusively masculine forms of speech in our references to the One whom we worship. Underneath the questions of grammar and syntax are the ethical issues of equality, freedom, the powers of men, and the rights of women. While justice and truth are much broader categories than those addressed in this book, these words are properly claimed here. What we say and do in the house of prayer does make claims about God and shape the structures of human existence.

How is the church responding to this challenge? Sometimes with bewilderment, then anger, reaction, embarrassed laughter, and condescending references to women, and occasional efforts to compensate with alternate liturgies. Or with much talk in classrooms and sacristies, in editorial offices and liturgical conferences. This conversation has given birth to private prayers and small group services that experiment with new liturgical forms. Some of these new forms of prayer are being tried in public worship, occasionally even the main Sunday service. The new worship books are being influenced by this challenge.[2]

Despite these initial responses, Christian public worship continues to be dominated by the metaphors of masculinity. On most Sundays I worship in churches of the extempore tradition, in which pastors develop the structure of the service and select or compose most of its hymns, devotions, and prayers. Week after week these services exhibit ignorance or ineptness—ignorance of the challenge or ineptness in devising ways of moving forward creatively. On other Sundays I worship in churches of the prayer book traditions, in which the text of the service is prescribed by church authority and published in official books. Whatever pastors may wish to do, they are bound by the disciplines of their churches to say what the books provide. On weekdays I worship in a seminary chapel, where the debate is more direct and intense. I know the pain of students and faculty, of men and women, of younger and older persons, as they joust with one another in the struggle to be true to their experiences and their understandings of reality.

While it is clear that liturgical language will be restructured, the detail of that reconstruction cannot yet be known. The dough is still rising and we do not know yet what the baked bread will be like. Even so, there is much that can now be done. Pastors, musicians, and other worship leaders can participate in the process, helping to prune old ways of their damaged parts, create new ways, and evaluate all in the effort to reform the language of worship.

The scene repeats itself so often that the actors and their lines are easily anticipated. The occasion is the meeting of the worship committee of a congregation. The actors include the minister, the choir director, and half a dozen other members of the congregation. The atmosphere is tense, feelings are high, and the committee's convener is having trouble keeping control. The previous Sunday the minister had rewritten the words of a well-known hymn and printed them in the bulletin, with the intention of getting around the masculine language that was so prominent in its text. The choir director was enraged: "It is not right to tamper with the words of a hymn, and besides you did it crudely. The meter was wrong and the rhyme was off." Before the minister could offer a defense, two women on the committee were sparring. Sitting boldly upright, her face flushed and her knuckles white, one woman declared that she didn't need to have any words changed. "I am proud to be a woman, and I know how the language works." Her antagonist applauded the minister's attempt at inclusive language, concluding her statement by saying, "It was the first Sunday in weeks that I could really worship."

Episodes like this reveal the complexity of the challenge to liturgical speech. Intertwined with theological and linguistic questions are other difficult topics, dealing with artistic standards, claims of law, interpersonal relations, local traditions, and the control of congregational life. No wonder feelings run high. Every one of these factors—convictions about God and religious authority, beliefs about right and wrong, the most basic principles of life in organized communities, personal power—is infused with emotional energy over which we have little control. Even when our minds understand and counsel patience, we are likely to find that another power within us takes control. We lash out with words that surprise us with their intensity and sharpness.

Therefore it is all the more important that we work with wisdom so that changes in the language of worship will draw us closer to God, lead us toward maturity in self-understanding and control, strengthen the church's witness to the gospel. The proposals that follow attempt to outline a pathway that leads through the thicket of linguistic and liturgical change. They are designed for pastors, musicians, and other worship leaders, for people who have to make decisions every week about what to say in the sanctuary. Although theoretical considerations lurk in the shadows, the form of this exposition is practical, aimed at helping people plan for next Sunday's service. I am making two assumptions: we have to go through this thicket, in this matter there is no choice; and we can choose our pathway. Surely there is a way that leads through the briars with only an occasional scratch. If we fail to find that pathway, we will be dragged through the center of the tangle, with clothing and flesh slashed by the thorny branches.

As I write, I am especially conscious of the fact that I (and most worship leaders) am male, middle-aged, and white. People like me created the liturgical tradition of the church and conduct its rites and ceremonies. We continue to dominate the chancels and sanctuaries of Christendom, the liturgical commissions, editorial offices, publishing houses, seminary classrooms, and agencies for the preservation of orthodoxy. Our bias seems inescapable, a persistent tendency toward conserving the past rather than creating a new future. It is hard for us even to be reformers of worship. To be revolutionaries is almost unthinkable. [3]

Yet I must speak—because so much of what I know about God is womanly. In the body of a woman I received the gift of life and at her breast I first experienced the numinous. From her stability throughout my childhood, I experienced the reality of the Rock upon whom the psalmists call, and by her way of transmitting freedom and responsibility, I discovered the meaning of my own authentic existence as a human being and as a man. Joined with another woman, I have gradually learned the fuller meaning of my manliness and have been granted the power of creating new life. The fruit of divine love, as it has been channeled through our bodies, includes three daughters each of whom has come to Christian womanhood. In fairness to these women, and to myself, it is important that I try to bring language and experience into closer correspondence with the truth of what we know of God and with the justice that befits our relations with one another.

Because justice and truth are such overwhelming words, it is necessary to approach them modestly. One component of justice is fairness, absolute fairness, rooted in God's own being, and therefore necessary for us. One aspect of truth is faithfulness, uncompromising faithfulness to our theological tradition and to our religious experience. Thus the first interim principle that can guide our striving for truth and justice in Christian worship is this: *during this transitional period our goal should be the development of liturgical language that is fair to women as well as to men and that is faithful to our experience of God.* As the discussion unfolds, I will suggest additional principles but this one stands out above the others. "Fairness" and "faithfulness" are the two words that help us find our directions.

All praise to you, O God our Savior.
As Creative Word, you give life and keep it strong,
    moment by moment sustaining us and calling us to faithfulness.
As living Commandment, you provide us with a pattern for life so
    that we can know how you want us to live and expect us to obey.
As suffering Servant, you show us your power of life
    and win the victory over sin.
As ever-present Spirit, you inspire us with the will to live according
    to your purposes.
O God our Savior, may you be praised!

Faithful and Fair

2

Love and Loyalty now meet,
Righteousness and Peace now embrace;
Loyalty reaches up from earth
and Righteousness leans down from heaven. (Ps. 85:10-11 JB)

One Sunday in August 1978 was a turning point in my understanding of the limitations of the traditional language of worship. Our oldest child was home for vacation after nearly two years of missionary service in Zaire. Before returning to her African labors, she preached in our church, the church where our family had worshiped for seventeen years, where she had made her confession of faith and been baptized, where she had often served as candlelighter and choir member, and where she had been commissioned for her work abroad.

In keeping with the occasion, our pastor chose a good missionary hymn, Mary A. Thompson's "O Zion, Haste, Thy Mission High Fulfilling." I sang energetically, joining in the call to "proclaim to every people, tongue, and nation / That God, in whom they live and move, is Love." Everything was fine until we reached the verse: "Give of thy sons to bear the message glorious." I knew what the hymn intended. After all, as professor I had explained that sort of thing before. The generic masculine use of sons should not confuse us. The hymn was challenging parents and congregations to inspire their own young people, both sons and daughters, to enter into missionary service, an intention I could fully support.

But Billie and I had "sent" not a son but a daughter—a woman with grace, charm, strength, and faith. With my head I knew that the hymn included her, but at the deeper level of my heart I wanted the hymn to proclaim that it was my daughter who had gone to publish glad tidings of peace, of Jesus, of redemption and release.

My discomfort that Sunday morning was relatively mild

compared to that which many people have experienced. Important as she is to me, my daughter is someone other than myself; the verbal slight did not touch the center of my own being. In seminary classes and in conversations, however, I hear the testimonies of people who encounter the exclusion directly and personally. Some of them have never heard the rules that govern the use of masculine words when persons in general are being referred to. Others know the rules in their heads but find that the vital center of self-identity overrules the rules. No matter what the conventions of language declare, women are left out. Left out when Christmas carols proclaim "peace on earth, good will to *men*." Left out when "good Christian *men*" are invited to "rejoice with heart and soul and voice." Left out when forced to call themselves *son* or *brother:* "Thou my great Father, I thy true *son*; / Thou in me dwelling and I with thee one"; "Time, like an ever-rolling stream, / Bears all its *sons* away"; "Lord, we thank thee for our *brothers*, / Keeping faith with us and thee."

Although all uses of masculine terms for persons in general or for groups made up of men and women may create confusion and pain, some practices are more troublesome than others. The more abstract the usage, the easier it is to bear; the more concrete, the harder to endure. When used to mean the human race, the word *man* is relatively clear . . . "good for man or beast." When used in plural forms, however, such words are confusing. "*Men* and children everywhere, / With sweet music fill the air." To whom does the word *men* refer? All human beings or adult males? Since children are specifically mentioned, *men* cannot mean all people (as distinguished from other living things). Probably the author means "adults and children," but the hymn is unclear. Not only does such language confuse meaning, but it contributes to the impression that the church belongs to men rather than to women and that God holds men in higher esteem than women.

Fair to All the People

These illustrations lead to the conclusion that generic language is not as clear as it is supposed to be. A growing body of literature reporting on empirical studies confirms the conclusion that every verbal transaction using masculine forms has to be interpreted.[1] In every instance we have to decide whether masculine words mean male persons only or human beings both male and female. The indicators are subtle: context, inflection, cultural habit, age of the persons involved, knowledge of conventional usage. When all parties to the verbal transaction are educated adults, with a well-developed knowledge of English usage, this process of interpretation often leads to agreement. It will be known whether the words in question refer only to males or to all persons.

Much of the time, however, the participants are not educated adults. They may be small children, or people with little schooling. Their English may be any of the many vernacular variants of the language. For them, these subtle indicators of meaning may pass unnoticed, with the result that meanings are obscured.

The studies are showing, however, that meaning is obscured even when participants are educated adults. The problems can be divided in two levels of seriousness. The one level might be called technical. Either meaning (males or persons) makes completely good sense, and nothing in the context indicates which it is. How does one decide? One shrugs one's shoulders and continues, assuming that sooner or later the truth will surface. Unfortunately, one party to the verbal transaction may decide too soon that the word means one or the other. The mistaken decision can lead to confusion and embarrassment, whether the decision is that the words mean males or that they refer to all persons regardless of sex.

The second level of seriousness is substantive. Often we form conclusions because our previous experiences condition us to understand things in only one way. I am still surprised when I see buses driven by women (and the surprise is even greater when I see the cockpit of an airliner under the control of a woman captain). Thus I am easily confused when I hear generic language used about bus drivers and pilots. "When a bus *driver* is on duty, *he* should . . ." Note that the noun does not indicate gender and that the masculine singular pronoun follows the normal pattern of generic language. But what comes to mind? Is it persons of either sex wearing a motor coach uniform? Or is it men? Despite my education and my knowledge of the language, including its use of masculine generic forms, I still think of males rather than of females and males. The puzzle that teases my mind is this: how are language and self-respect linked together? Has English developed in this way because society has already been stratified according to sex? Or has society become stratified because the language itself is biased toward men and against women? It is clear that language patterns do shape some aspects of social structure. We draw certain conclusions because of the form of statements even though the intrinsic content of the statements may not intend what we concluded.

In our Christian literature this problem of confusion is illustrated by material dealing with ministers. Hymns and other writings often used masculine forms to refer to ministers, as in the verse "God of the prophets! / Bless the prophets' sons." Does this author, Denis Wortman, mean young people as is the clear intention in "O Zion, Haste"? Or does he mean young men? My guess is that he means to refer to males. Wortman wrote it for the centennial celebration of New Brunswick Seminary in October, 1884, and in his accompanying letter refers to "all loyal sons" of the seminary. [2] At that time seminarians were exclusively male, as were ministers in most churches, Catholic and Protestant.

Thus Wortman's usage is not intended to be generic. He intended to refer to males. Yet the form duplicates generic use, implying that prophets as a class will always be male. *Sonship* may be physical or spiritual. It includes the younger generation—sons, nephews, "Timothys," and all the others. Yet even this extension of the language to a partially generic use implies that all representatives of the class *minister* will be male. The hymn that started out as a description of seminary life has become a means of strengthening a particular understanding of the way that ministry is supposed to be.

Here I am not discussing whether or not the ministry should include both women and men (which I believe it should). The only point I want to make here is that the form of Wortman's hymn leads to a specific conclusion concerning this matter. It assumes a position by means of a literary form; but our beliefs about the ministry should be made not on the basis of the accidents of poetry but as the result of careful biblical study and theological discussion. For Christians the discussion about language is more than a search for clarity and precision, important as these values are. Theological principles concerning human life and the forms of human community are even more important. Through the generations of time, our race has been struggling to achieve the fullness intended by God since the creation. For every forward movement, there seems to be a recoil so that progress is slow, jagged, often marked by regression. Even so, the goal is clear and the direction unmistakable.

The one biblical statement that expresses this vision with absolute clarity is Paul's evangelical declaration: "For as many of you as were baptized into Christ have put on Christ. There is neither Jew nor Greek, there is neither slave nor free, there is neither male nor female; for you are all one in Christ Jesus" (Gal. 3:27-28). It is doubtful that even Paul understood the full import of this declaration which came as the crescendo of a rhetorical pronouncement concerning the relationship of the law and the gospel. His chief interest was the debate between Christians of Jewish ethnicity and those of gentile blood, a debate which Paul resolved by declaring that all Christians are Abraham's offspring, heirs according to God's promise, true children of God. The principle which he declared is that our identity in Christ overcomes the old divisions that have split apart the human race—divisions of race and nationality, of social class and station in life, of sex. In Christ, Paul claims, all have been given a new equality.

In his further work Paul seemed able to develop consistently one of these categories, the one of race and nationality. Here his mind was clear and his policies forthright. The church would be a united community that lived beyond the divisions of language, culture, and race. Often he was consistent in his teachings about class and social condition. Certainly Paul was right when he condemned the Corinthians for bringing their class structure into the place of worship and letting it divide the congregation into rich and poor, slave and free. (See I Cor. 11.) His Letter to Philemon is clear in its intent, which is to establish a new form of equality between two men who had been slave owner and slave but now are made equal in Christ Jesus.

With respect to women and men, Paul was less clear. Perhaps he had not intended to be so sweeping in his declaration; yet the logic is right, and so is his passion. This ancient division is also meant to be overcome in a new Christian equality and unity. In some of his pastoral directions, such as I Corinthians 11 and 14, Paul distinguishes between women and men in ways that undercut his evangelical vision. Yet personal comments at the close of his letters reveal the fact that his circle of very close colleagues and workers included women. See especially Romans 16.[3]

The history of the church is disheartening with respect to the gospel vision of human equality in Jesus Christ. The divisions which Christ has overcome continue to shatter the human community . . . race and nationality, social class and position, and sex divide us into the powerful and the powerless, the privileged and the deprived. Most pervasive of all has been the subjugation of women because this division has taken place in every race and human class. Even the recent history of Western Christianity shows this flopping back and forth between a new humanity in Christ and the old humanity divided into status and condition.

This vacillation is illustrated by the participation of women in the missionary movement of the late nineteenth and early twentieth centuries.[4] Missionary boards were developed by women and provided the opportunity for women to act independently and with full responsibility. Much of the classical era of Protestant missions is the direct outgrowth of this aggressive work by women both in the mission boards at home and in the fields of missionary service abroad. Despite this period of remarkable advance there have been very serious setbacks and these as recently as in the half century ending about 1965. In the church and in Western society as a whole this period was marked by two developments: the gradual collapse of formal barriers to the participation of women in the positions that society gave them permission to enter and the gradual reduction in the proportion of women serving in these positions. Although I have lived through a portion of this period of reversal, I was but dimly aware of what was taking place. Only after reading historical accounts and interpretations, have I been able to comprehend the pattern of what I have actually experienced.

Although my illustrations have come from the language and history of the church, this issue extends far beyond the church. Writers in other fields are insisting that the ways we use the language must change so that clarity and equality are its characteristics.[5] Verbal instructions are to say what they mean and give the two sexes the same status. Language is no longer to serve as an instrument whereby women are kept in subordinate positions and men in places of superiority. The need for fairness cuts both ways. Traditional patterns of speech cause trouble for men, too. Their vision is blocked, their understanding cramped, their capacity to act shackled. They develop false perceptions of their own importance and preeminence. As a result of social conditioning they too are locked into patterns of activity that may be demeaning to themselves and to others.

Some people are not aware of the injustice that current uses of language inflict. For these people the old ways have worked well and continue to do so, but their number is diminishing. Younger persons especially, impatient with the older usage, are rightly demanding that the language change. And I have seen in Sunday school classes and in churches where I've preached that a surprising number of older persons are also happy to see patterns altered. They may start out by saying that they have no trouble with masculine forms since they are secure in their womanly identities, yet some of these older women have moved to the edge of their chairs, with a fiery look in their eyes, when I have talked about this subject. The need for clear and equal language crosses the barriers between the generations.

Faithful to God

Whereas we have been aware of the *people-talk* challenge for quite some time, the *God-talk* challenge has only recently entered the church's consciousness. We thought we knew how to talk to God and about God . . . and the language of hymnody, prayers, and systematic theology all expressed this confidence. My own confidence (might I say complacency) was broken open when several students interrupted one of my lectures on the language of prayer. I had been discussing the use of you and your instead of *thee* and *thou*. When I mentioned that some writers were also questioning the masculinity of liturgical language, the debate broke out. On the one side, some students argued that masculinity expresses the very nature of God. God is called He, Father, and King, they insisted, because these words give us a truer insight into God's reality than their feminine counterparts can do. Later one of these students told me that he knows this language to be figurative, that God does not have sex organs and is father to humanity in a way that is different from the way that men become fathers of their children. Even so, this student insisted, we have to use masculine language because only these forms of speech communicate faithful insights into the divine nature.

Other students in that class session claimed that all human speech about God is figurative, that we never experience God's fullness, and that no human idea, no human language is capable of expressing God's character. They insisted that even the name Father is a metaphor, a word that ought not to be taken literally when used in reference to God. It became clear that these members of the class not only wanted to affirm that old language is figurative, but also they wanted to develop additional metaphors, including some that are feminine. If we can call God Father, they asked, then why not Mother too?

The debate was not resolved that day in class, not for those students, nor for other church people in their houses of worship; nor has it been settled for any of us in our public speech about God. Instead, new questions have forced themselves into our discussions and debates, into our prayers and our theologies. Who is God? Can human speech ever describe divinity faithfully and truthfully? What is the authority of the Bible for our worship, how binding are biblical language and forms? What is the source of liturgical language? What criteria are to be used in evaluating the words spoken when we pray?

At this point in our struggle with liturgical language we are much like Moses who, on the day he saw the burning bush, called out to the Lord, What will I tell the people when they ask me the name of the God who has sent me? His question was urgent for two reasons: he had to know the true identity of the mysterious Voice who was sending him on so dangerous a mission; and the people would test Moses' reliability by the way he named this God. Both issues are still important and lie back of the debate over the language of prayer. We too want to be assured that the voices we hear come from the one God, revealed by Jesus Christ. And the people to whom we are sent demand that our teachings be faithful to this same revelation.

It is significant that Moses demanded a name, and that God answered in a way that shortcircuited the request. Instead of giving a name, God said: "I AM WHO I AM. . . . Say this to the people of Israel, 'I AM has sent me to you'" (Exod. 3:14). [6] This "name" which is spelled YHWH is really no name at all. Instead, it is a play on words, a cryptic set of letters derived from the Hebrew verb which means "to be." The meaning of this name is debated, but the most prominent opinions stress the active, present, causative qualities. YHWH "is the One who causes to be what is (or what happens)," in whose sovereign will "historical events and natural happenings have their origin." The God who spoke to Moses is *being itself*, the principle and power of all that is; and for that reason, if we must have a name for God, it will be one that expresses this connection between being and the One whose very self being is.

Certainly the Hebrews knew to whom the word pointed. It identified the one true God who had created the earth, sent the flood, and saved Noah. This namelike set of letters referred to the God who had called Abraham from Ur of Chaldea, promised him descendants as many as the sand of the sea, and destroyed Sodom and Gomorrah. It pointed out the God who had sent Joseph to Egypt and had protected the people from the famine. And now this same God had come to Moses, promising that the people could escape from their slavery and return to their ancestral home. Although the Hebrews used other titles for God, this name given to Moses was the only real name of their God. In the Old Testament this name YHWH appears some 6,700 times, more than all the other titles of God combined.

The most common term from the general culture available to the Hebrews was the general word for god. Semites around them talked of *El*, but Hebrews ordinarily used this word for deity in combination with modifying words. *El Shaddai* was the most important alternative to YHWH, and originally may have meant God of the Mountains. It came to express the majesty and omnipotence of YHWH. *El-elyon* meant Exalted One or Most High. Another combination, *El Olam*, seems to mean *Everlasting One*. *Elohim*, though plural in form, was usually understood to be singular and stressed "the fact that God, the Creator, is the absolute Lord over his creation and the sovereign of history."[7]

The people knew this God to be powerful and arbitrary, given to wrath as well as to mercy—definitely a divine being to treat with respect. Even the divine name, YHWH, had to be treated with respect—respect so great that it could not be pronounced. When people came to the letters which spelled God's personal name, they always said something else: instead of pronouncing it (the letters might have sounded like *Yahweh*)—instead of saying I AM WHO I AM—they would say the word for lord. Their eyes would see YHWH and their mouths would say *Adonai*.

One conclusion which can be drawn from this discussion of the divine name is that it makes a very great difference what we call God. Names are direct links between us and the persons, including God, with whom we deal. Names display character and portray attitudes. They can be used in ways that bless and damn. Names give life and they also destroy. A second conclusion is that God is never tied to names, even to the name given to Moses at the burning bush. No matter what the name, God is greater than the names, always more complex than the names can account for. No matter how much our names may express God's nature, there is more to God than our names can begin to say.

Because of their strong sense of God's nearness and God's awesomeness, Hebrews developed other ways of referring to the God whose name they dared not pronounce. Just as family members and close friends create nicknames and terms of endearment for those whom they love, so did the devout men and women of Israel. One

which became increasingly important was *Father* (Ps. 68:5; 89:26;
Isa. 63:16; 64:8), and it was this term of endearment and respect
which Jesus used as his most frequent way of addressing God. He
taught his disciples to use this family word in their prayers, too.
Indeed, Father has for Christians become another name for God.
Yet even Father tells only part of what God really is like, a fact
which we know from our normal experiences with people. One man
is known in so many ways, and the names we use reveal multiple
facets of his personality. His small children call him Father, but so
does his wife . . . the same name but such different meanings. He is
called by his personal name, but even that name means different
things, depending upon who uses it and with what inflection. There
are special names that depict certain periods of his life and reveal
specific dimensions of his character. Even yet I remember the
strange feeling that came over me as a small boy the first time I heard
my mother speak of my father with the nickname of his earlier years,
the name by which she had first known him but now rarely used, a
name that spoke of a past that I did not share, of a life that I would
never know.

Thus our own experience with names on the human level
confirms the Hebrew respect for the name of God. Names are
powerful signs of life and personality. They are to be used with full
awareness of their potency. Yet no name tells all there is to be told; no
name reveals all the qualities and characteristics of a person's life and
character.

The many names and titles that develop in our relationships with
God indicate that the divine personality is highly complex. Although
the Jewish-Christian tradition has stressed that God is one (see Deut.
6:4 and Eph. 4:6), certain parts of the sacred writings speak as though
God is known to us in several guises, each of which expresses some
part of the divine personality. In his classic study of this tendency,
Helmer Ringgren cites three reasons.[8] One of these causes is rooted
in ancient Semitic thought—a tendency toward concretization. The
second is the influence of Egyptian religion to personify the
attributes of God. The third tendency came from Greece, which was
to use separate titles for the attributes and functions of deity.

The strongest expression of this tendency in the Old Testament is Proverbs 8 and 9 where Wisdom is personified and described in godlike language. Similar passages are to be found in contemporaneous writings that are not included in canonical scripture, especially Ben Sirach 24:1-31 and Wisdom of Solomon 7:22–8:1. Three aspects of Wisdom are especially important as she is described in Proverbs. Perhaps most important is the fact that Wisdom is distinguished from the One whose name is Yahweh. Wisdom was created by the Lord at the very beginning of God's work of creation. Because she was created, Wisdom clearly is subordinate to Yahweh; but at the same time Wisdom is superior to everything else. A second characteristic is that Wisdom assisted in the work that God did, "Then I was beside him, like a master workman" (Prov. 8:30). The third characteristic is that Wisdom is feminine gender. In an inflected language gender and sex are different categories. Many nouns that cannot be considered female are grammatically feminine. The interesting question, therefore, is whether the feminine gender in this instance is merely a grammatical accident, or is it instead a deliberate choice of words based on insight into God's character?

The puzzle is complicated by the fact that certain other Old Testament words also are ascribed to God as though they were personifications of God's attributes. Some are feminine and some are masculine. Ringgren calls special attention to Righteousness and Peace—Sedek and Salem. "Righteousness and peace will kiss each other" (Ps. 85:10b). Here the tendency toward personification is more restrained than with Wisdom. Indeed, it is not at all clear that sedek and salem were ever anything other than abstract moral qualities in the tradition of the Hebrews.

Another word that more clearly stands distinct is spirit—ruah. This Spirit moved over the waters at creation (Gen. 1:2), and is in some sense separable from the Lord because it can enter into persons (Judg. 11:29; Ps. 51:11; Ezek. 2:2), and is free to travel about. In the New Testament, Spirit continues to be described with the language of deity (Eph. 4:30).

Neither Jews nor Christians knew what to do with these

personifications of God. In the Old Testament they are suppressed enough that it is possible to overlook their presence. In the New Testament, however, this suppressed multiplicity of God's character becomes much more prominent. Much of what the Hebrews had meant by wisdom was transferred to the Greek word *logos* and then ascribed to Jesus. Spirit continued her ambiguous course through piety and theology. Ever since then systematic theology has been working at the task of explaining how the *logos*, incarnate in Jesus, and the Spirit are related to the one God.[9]

In the movement from Hebrew to Greek, from *hokhmah* to *logos*, two things happen. The idea of subordination is lost. Jesus as the Word is more closely the equivalent of God than Wisdom had been. And the feminine gender is lost; *logos* is a masculine word and Jesus was a male. Once established in early Christian life, these two tendencies were later continued and given fixed forms in worship and theology. The Christian God is perceived officially in three manifestations, all of which have been considered masculine. We pray to and discuss God the Father, Son, and Holy Spirit.

Yet this consensus does not seem to remain in place. We continue to define and redefine trinitarian thought; and other characteristics of God persistently rise up in piety, liturgy, and theology.

The principle which supports this discussion is that language is faithful to God when it correctly identifies the one true God who from the beginning has been creating and sustaining, judging and showing mercy, hiding in the secret processes of nature and going public in the lives of saints and the words of prophets.

At this point we can ask two questions: (1) does our conventional liturgical language accurately point to the God of Abraham, David, Isaiah, and Jesus? And to the God of Miriam, Ruth, Bathsheba, Mary, and Dorcas? (2) is it possible that new language will develop which will help us speak more faithfully of the one true God whose personal name is too sacred to pronounce?

For some time now I have been especially attentive to the way people, including myself, pray in public. I am appalled at the emptiness of much liturgical language, at its dullness, its vain repetitions. Although these problems sometimes appear in books of services and prayers, they are even more prevalent in extempore prayers, both in church and in other Christian gatherings. There is an apparent mindlessness that suggests shallow religious life and skimpy preparation for the leading of public prayer. Therefore I want to answer the two questions in the above paragraph by saying that the time has come for us to reexamine longstanding habits. Some church customs which have served us well in the past need to be set aside. New forms of speech need to be developed. The language of prayer is flexible and responsive to our experiences of God. The time has come for a new burst of creativity—and of truth.

Blessing and glory,
wisdom, thanksgiving, and honor,
power and might,
are yours, O God our Savior.
We join our voices with the multitude of the redeemed,
with the angels and the creatures of heaven
who stand around your throne praising you.
With them, we yearn for that time when
    all creation will be brought to its perfection,
    when we will be sheltered by your presence,
    when people will no longer suffer hunger or thirst,
    when the sun will no longer attack with scorching heat,
    when you will wipe away all tears from our eyes.
Then will we join in the song of everlasting adoration, crying out:
    "Salvation belongs to you, O God,
    and to the Lamb who was slain for us."

Sovereignty and Intimacy

3

*The Lord says, ". . . You will be like a child that is
nursed by its mother, carried in her arms, and treated with love.
I will comfort you . . . as a mother comforts her child." (Isa. 66:12-13
TEV)*

Experience and language are intertwined, the one shaping the other. They form an alternating current—first experience of the divine, then the effort to respond in words, then renewed and subtly altered experience with God. The church seems most of the time to be in the language phase. There are brief periods of heightened awareness of God—certain episodes in the Bible, the Reformation of the sixteenth century, the Wesley revivals, and a few other episodes—followed by long periods of time during which these encounters with God are reexperienced through the words and music of worship and theology.

What I am calling dullness in contemporary worship may be a sign that the cycle is about to reverse itself, swinging away from the language phase to the renewal of the experiential phase. If so, a special mode of consciousness is what we need, a disciplined form of relaxation which makes it possible for us to renew our own experiences of the major aspects of God's character. Temporarily freed from the constraints of conventional rules of public prayer, we can savor other ways of approaching God and calling on the Holy One.[1] New patterns of language can then arise, transcending current orthodoxies, because they express new appropriations of our experience of the divine. The interim principle guiding us during this part of the process can be stated this way: *during this transitional period there should be a deliberate and determined effort to extend the metaphorical foundation of the speech used to describe and address God.*

The Dazzling Light of the Lord's Presence

On a sun-drenched day in late spring, I visited a large, new orthodox church high on a hill looking over San Francisco Bay. The building itself was a massive white dome, and the vast entrance court was paved in white. The late morning sun, reflecting from this unbroken expanse of white, hurt my eyes. Although the inside of the church was quite dim, the copper-colored sheathing on walls and dome reflected hundreds of candles and small incandescent lamps so that the worship space seemed alive with light. Here, in the middle part of the twentieth century, in one of the most secularized American cities, it was possible to sense the majesty of the Lord God Almighty.

The mood expressed in the architecture of that building is very much like the mood expressed in the literary imagery of the Psalter and Revelation. Sometimes the dramatic elements of a mountain storm are used as metaphor to suggest God's glory. The servant of God in Psalm 18, in dangerous circumstances, called on God for deliverance and was answered by the Most High at whose anger the earth reeled and rocked, the foundations of the mountains trembling and quaking. This prayer poem tells of smoke coming from God's nostril and devouring fire from God's mouth. The passage is heavily laden with references to wings of the wind, thick darkness, hailstones, coals of fire, arrows, lightnings, convulsions of land and sea. This experience of God's person and presence includes grandeur, unbridled power, drama, splendor. One translation uses the phrase "the dazzling light of the Lord's presence" (Exod. 33:17-23; 40:34-38 TEV) to express the majesty and glory of God.

Another vision of God is the central motif of the last book of the Bible. John the Elder strains language to portray the glory of God enthroned in heaven. John heaps up images: precious substances of jasper, carnelian, and emeralds; flashes of lightning, voices and peals of thunder; seven torches of fire; a sea of glass like crystal. The throne of God is surrounded by twenty-four lesser thrones, each with an elder seated, clothed in a white garment with a golden crown upon his head. The heavenly retinue is completed with four remarkable creatures, full of eyes all around and within, who day and night never cease to sing:

> "Holy, holy, holy, is the Lord God Almighty,
> who was and is and is to come!" (Rev. 4:8)

The elders join the living creatures in this ceaseless hymn of praise, casting their crowns before the throne, singing:

> "Worthy art thou, our Lord and God,
> to receive glory and honor and power,
> for thou didst create all things,
> and by thy will they existed and were created." (Rev. 4:11)
>   See Revelation 4:1-11.

Much of the language of worship throughout the full history of the people of God expresses this experience of the One who is glorious, majestic, clothed in light inexpressible. Liturgies of the Eastern churches seem especially attentive to this aspect of God's self-disclosure, but Western Christians have expressed it too.[2] God's glory continues to be the source of titles and ascriptions in hymns, prayers, and sermons.

This experience of divine glory divides in two kinds of language, both of which assert that God's majesty is more powerful than all the powers that overwhelm persons in their lives. Some figures of speech are drawn from nature, others from the political realm. God is sovereign over nature, long ago creating cosmos out of chaos, but also coming to us in the voice of the whirlwind (Job 38:1) and in the silence after storms (I Kings 19:9-14). The message of the prophets is that God's power over kings and empires is absolute, causing some to rise up and others to be destroyed.

If our language of prayer is to be faithful to this vision of the majestic God, we need to use a richer vocabulary than the title Lord, which is true but very limited. We Christians, however, may find it difficult to develop this richer vocabulary because our devotion to Jesus has diminished our awareness of the God who sent him to us. This emphasis upon the *Incarnate One* rather than the *Transcendent One* is foreshadowed in the prologue to the Epistle to the Hebrews where the author says that in these last days God has spoken to us by a Son who has been appointed "the heir of all things, through whom also he created the world." This Son "reflects the glory of God and bears the very stamp of his nature, upholding the universe by his word of power." Having completed his work of making purification for sins, this Son "sat down at the right hand of the Majesty on high" (Heb. 1:1-4). What has happened in the years since then is that prayers and hymns assign dynamic and active attributes to Jesus, leaving the static elements as the continuing attributes of God who is the sovereign of nature and history.

An ancient hymn by Ambrose (d. 396) shows how the attributes of God's glory are assigned to Jesus, the Anointed One. "O splendor of God's glory bright, / O thou that bringest light from light, / O Light of light, light's living spring, / O day, all days illumining." Another hymn, also addressed to Jesus, illustrates the same tendency, ascribing to him God's majestic sovereignty over nature and history. "Fairest Lord Jesus, / Ruler of all nature, / O thou of God and man the son, / Thee will I cherish, / Thee will I honor, / Thou, my soul's glory, joy, and crown." Note, in contrast, the static character of God the Creator in the hymn by Joseph Addison: "The spacious firmament on high, / With all the blue ethereal sky, / And spangled heavens, a shining frame, / Their great Original proclaim: / Th' unwearied sun, from day to day, / Does his creator's power display, / And publishes to every land / The work of an almighty hand." A later stanza tells of the silence of the universe and then affirms of the moon, stars, and planets that "In reason's ear they all rejoice, / And utter forth a glorious voice; / Forever singing, as they shine, / 'The hand that made us is divine.'" While it is right that we adore Jesus our Savior, this devotion to the Incarnate One ought not to be at the expense of the Transcendent One whose majesty continues to be expressed over nature and history.

From Experience to Language

The dazzling light of the Lord's presence! The essential inspiration of all liturgical language . . . yet so far from the regular experience of Christians in the major churches of the West. The crucial questions are, Is it possible for people like us to be flooded by this divine light? Are there ways for ministers, musicians, and other worship leaders to be rekindled with the divine fire?

These questions are especially important in the broad band of middle American churches—acculturated, aging, pleasant, and diminishing. In these churches the Hebrew God of fire and light seems far away. We read about this God and are not quite sure how to respond because the contrast between the Holy One of Israel and the God we hear about in our churches is so great. A quarter century ago, when I first came across Evelyn Underhill's sensuous and concentrated study on worship, I had to push the book away, so strange to me was her vision of God; and students with backgrounds similar to mine continue to repeat that rejection. In time, I (and some of my students) have come closer to Underhill's Hebraic God, to this dazzling light of majesty and power.[3] Even so, congregations on Sunday seem so tepid. Our youth grow up scarcely touched, rarely singed by the divine fire. They still claim to believe, if we can accept the studies reported by current sociologists of religion, but they do not belong.[4]

There are some, however, who, like Peter Jenkins, are caught up in this dazzling light. Young, white, college-educated, jaded, fed up with himself and life in America, he started on a walk across the country, determined to give America one last chance. When his money ran out he wintered with a black family in Texana, on the edge of Murphy, North Carolina. One condition laid down by the mother of the family was that he go to Mount Zion Baptist Church with them every Sunday. The reluctance with which he went that first Sunday was swept away by a religious vitality that his previous years in a Connecticut church had never provided. Always before, church had been "a dead place where you were expected to sit still through a thirty- or forty-minute monotone sermon about social ethics." Before Mount Zion, he had been turned on only by rock concerts, but worship in this church "made Woodstock and a Stevie Wonder concert at Fillmore East in New York City seem as boring as waiting for school to end on a hot June day." Later in this same journey, Peter attended a revival in Mobile. The preacher began his sermon: "I'm not going to keep you long, but I want to talk to you tonight about God." Later in the sermon, the preacher's words penetrated Peter's inner life: "The deepest corners of my being were lit with thousand-watt light bulbs. . . . All of me was exposed in God's searchlight."[5] This was the same God, Peter decided, that they worshiped at Mount Zion.

Other people today experience the encounter with God in ways that have transformed their lives. For some it has happened in conservative churches as it did for Peter Jenkins. For others, it has been in Catholic churches, and it also takes place in mainline Protestant churches. Some people have encountered the dazzling light of the Lord's presence in apparent separation from any churchly contact.

One factor is clear, however. These experiences of encounter with God take place one by one or in relatively small numbers. We are not in a period of mass movements toward faith, when the population as a whole is overwhelmed by religious experience. Ours is not a time of a new "great awakening."

For most of us, at least in the mainline churches, the renewed experience of God will come from the inside rather than from the outside. Rather than being swept up by a new Jonathan Edwards who overpowers the culture as a whole, we will be fired by the religious energy that lies dormant in daily experience . . . in our struggles with the natural world, in our close dealings with other people, in our fears and hopes, our hates and our loves. God meets us when we are overtaken by any experience that transcends our power to understand or control and yet must be dealt with some way.

We do meet God, even in this secularized and seemingly nonreligious period of time. The task for ministers and musicians is to find ways of identifying this experience and then of expressing it in our prayers and services. The Divine Majesty is still present in human life and we need new ways of putting it into liturgical words and actions.

Since this is a book about worship, I must set aside further discussion of congregational life and church program, with the acknowledgment that there is much to be said. Here, I must concentrate on liturgical issues only. For Christians in the mainstream of Western culture, the key to the recovery of religious vitality is in the liturgy—in the words and actions of worship.

What I am discovering in my own liturgical life is that the closer I come to the ancient and authentic tradition of prayer, the easier it is to find language that transcends the sexist bias of the liturgical speech with which I grew up.

You Are Praised, O Lord Our God

One source of help is the large body of liturgical material found in modern Jewish worship, rooted as it is in the same ancient soil as is Christian prayer and praising the same God. Although Jewish liturgical life, like Christian, has evolved through the centuries, it can help Christians in three ways. Jewish prayer expresses God's active sovereignty as well as the "once and for all time" aspects of what God did long ago. It uses patterns of formulas which lend themselves to Christian prayer and which can free our imaginations from the chains that hold us captive. Prayers of the synagogue also contain many phrases and figures of speech that can be carried over into the prayers of the church.[6]

One Hebraic prayer pattern, present in the Bible and expanded through the years, was adopted by Christians early in the church's life, probably forming the inspiration for the first prayers at the Lord's Table. Like most formulas, this pattern is tightly organized, but its value is that it simultaneously frees the imagination and protects the prayer's theological integrity. Originally, this prayer pattern had two parts, says Joseph Heinemann, and was used to express brief, extempore prayers.[7] The first part, *the proclamation*, was stable, unchanging in its content even though it did permit certain additions. Although the main clause can be translated several ways, "blessed be the Lord," or "praise be to God" indicate the intentions of the Hebrew phrase. This naming of God could be expanded with an adjectival phrase such as "Most High" or "the God of Israel." The second part of the pattern, the main content clause, is active, expressing the reason why God is to be praised. An ancient example of this prayer form is the expression of praise uttered by Abraham's servant: "Blessed be the Lord, the God of my master Abraham, who has not forsaken his steadfast love and his faithfulness toward my master" (Gen. 24:27).

Over time this formula was expanded, says Heinemann. The proclamation remained much as it had always been, with the addition of the word "you." The main clause was often enlarged to become hymn-like recitations of God's actions, both in the past and in current life. This declaration of thanksgiving became the basis for petitions for God's future action. The expanded form of this prayer pattern included a second blessing that closed the prayer with an echo of its opening proclamation. A modern example of the full form of this prayer pattern is a text taken from a service for Yom Kippur:

> Praised be the Lord our God and God of all generations, God of our mothers and fathers, of Abraham, Isaac, and Jacob, Sarah, Rebekah, Rachel, and Leah, great, mighty and exalted.
> *You bestow love and kindness on all Your children. You remember the devotion of our ancestors. In Your love, You bring redemption to their descendants for the sake of Your name.*
> Remember us unto life, O King, who delights in life, and inscribe us in the Book of Life, for Your sake, O God of life.
> *You are our Ruler and our Helper, our Savior and Protector. Blessed is our Eternal God, Shield of our people in every age.*[8]

These four sections of the blessing formula can be outlined as follows:

a) Proclamation (of praise to God)
b) Declaration (of thanksgiving for an action or attribute of God)
c) Petition (for God's future action)
d) Benediction (an echo of the opening praise of God)

One of the values of this pattern as a stimulus to our liturgical creativity can be seen when we concentrate on the second element, the declaration of thanksgiving. Devout people experience the miracle of God's presence and power everywhere, although they often do not think about life in this religious way. Thus, a wide range of experience can become the body of this declaration; or, changing the figure, these varied experiences become the engine that drives this prayer. For example, a prayer for Rosh Hashana praises God "who has made our bodies with wisdom, combining veins, arteries, and vital organs in a finely balanced system." This declaration is preceded by the proclamation "Blessed is our Eternal God, Creator of the universe," and followed by an echoing benediction: "Wondrous Fashioner and Sustainer of life, Source of our health and strength, we give You thanks and praise."[9] The prayer is thematically united because the beginning and ending proclaim the divine attributes which we experience and express in the declaration of thanksgiving.

So much can determine the thanksgiving: moments in personal religious experience, significant episodes in the life of congregations and communities, events in the larger worlds of culture and politics. Our experiences of the natural world become proper elements for the thanksgiving—its grandeur and awesomeness, its beauty and delight, its mystery. All these aspects of life help us praise God; and they help us find a constant succession of new titles and ascriptions. There will be certain often-used ascriptions—creator, maker, ruler, sovereign, giver, source. Often these titles will be modified by adjectives or participial phrases—for example, glorious Creator, Creator of beginnings, Eternal God, God of all generations. Synonymns may appear: "Praised be the Power that brings renewal to the soul, the vital song that makes creation dance!"[10] Once we grasp the vital connection between life's experience and the attributes of God, our imaginations are freed and the language of prayer is greatly extended.

Over the years that I have prepared prayers for public worship, my work has been stimulated by meditating on two kinds of human experience, both of them common to all people. We are preoccupied with weather and the conditions outside and my prayers have praised God for the warmth of the sun, the colors of the earth, the productivity of the fields, the power of wind and rain, the glory of autumn leaves, the puritan fire of ice, the smells of spring . . . the list goes on and on. I sometimes worry for fear that there is too great a preoccupation in my prayers with these passing episodes of the natural world, until I remember that Jesus also drew upon this source for his public utterances.

People also are preoccupied with the common ventures of their lives—sickness and health, frustration and confidence, indifference and love, tragedy and hope. I find myself brooding over recent episodes and letting these well up in carefully composed references to such moments of experience. These are offered to God as causes for praise, reasons for confession, or the substance of petitions.

Many of the titles for God that result from this process are very strong images, both in their ideas and their emotional content. Furthermore, many of them are what grammarians might call common gender, specifying neither male nor female. Thus, they transcend the problem of deciding whether to use male or female terms to describe God. These reflections help us enlarge our vocabulary of titles for God in a way that is filled with the language of wonder, mystery, and divine fullness.

I have concentrated on the second part of the Jewish prayer formula because it moves us toward the vital center of piety, the specific and concrete experiences in which the shape, flavor, sound, aroma, and texture of the divine come to us. Much of the power of liturgical life is generated in these experiences. There is, however, the other side of prayer, the abstract and general way of summing up and interpreting what we meet in the specific experiences of every day. The first element of the Jewish pattern is where this abstract dimension of our liturgical theology expresses itself. Here we use carefully constructed words and phrases to state the essence of what we know God to be. Again, the range of language available to us is much greater than many leaders of worship have realized.

Some of the literature of prayer displays the possibilities for extending this part of our liturgical language. One example that is especially stimulating is the work of Theodore Parker, who more than a century ago electrified Boston with his bold preaching on the major issues of the day. He also ministered to Boston's deepest needs by prayers of remarkable tenderness and scope. One of his leading ideas was that God is "the Infinite of Power, Wisdom, Justice, Love, whereon we may repose, wherein we may confide."[11] Consistent with this belief, Parker's prayers address God with terms based on that conception. Frequently Parker started a paragraph (his prayers were long) with the phrase, "O Thou Infinite One," to which he attached a relative clause describing some way in which this general characteristic of God is expressed with immediacy and power: ". . . who art amidst all the silences of nature, and forsakest us not with thy spirit . . ." (p. 33); ". . . who fillest the ground under our feet and the heavens over our head . . ." (p. 38); ". . . who dwellest not only in temples made with hands, but art a perpetual presence, living and moving and having thy being in every star that flowers above and every flower that flames beneath . . ." (p. 69).

Parker often used a similar formula but with other phrasing: "O Thou Infinite Spirit" (p. 44); "O Thou Infinite Power" (p. 59); "O Thou Perpetual Presence" (p. 64). Regularly this abstract and general title of God was wedded to concrete and particular experiences. In a prayer offered in May, he moves quickly to thank the Infinite One for "the footsteps of Spring throughout our Northern land, giving new vigor to the cattle's grass, and causing hope to spring up with the farmer's slow-ascending corn" (p. 65). After addressing God as "Almighty Power, All-present Spirit, . . . All-knowing Wisdom, and All-righteous Justice," Parker praises this infinity of all powers who "hast thine arms around this dusty world, this spiritual sphere, and the souls of good men made perfect." He concludes this portion of his prayer by thanking God "for the motherly care wherewith thou watchest over every living thing which thou hast created . . ." (pp. 145-46).

Because current liturgical use has abandoned the archaic thou, we cannot duplicate Parker's pattern. As a term of personal address, "O Thou Infinite Power" is both reverent and clear. If we change thou to you, however, the phrase loses both reverence and clarity. If we drop the first two words and use only the phrase "Infinite Power," the term recovers a portion of its strength, but still seems to be bare. If spoken with sufficient warmth of manner and appropriate vocal qualities, this simple and barren phrase could be a strong invocation of God.

Another way of adapting this approach is to address God directly, placing the descriptive phrase in apposition: O God, Infinite Power. A modification of this same pattern is to supply words that explain the comma: O God, you are Infinite Justice. Still another pattern is to insert these terms of divine address into the proclamation (the first part of the Jewish formula described above): Praise be to you, O God, Perpetual Presence; or, Infinite One, let your name be praised.

Because the titles of God described in this section are abstract and general, they challenge the liturgical imagination to fill in the specification that gives them life. When we are composing prayers, we can ask questions such as: How does God who is Infinite Power energize life as we know it? How does God express the Infinite Justice which is part of the divine character? How does the Infinite Love, which is central to God's own nature, touch our lives? The main body of the prayer becomes the answer to these questions, reciting specific ways in which the Infinite One comes to us, infuses us, and energizes us.

Intimacy

Sovereignty and infinity are such austere ways of approaching God and expressing the many qualities of the divine character. Even with all the warm, pleasing, and immediate experiences of God's majesty and perfection, we still are kept at a distance. Therefore, we eagerly claim one more pathway to God, one more way of understanding the One who gives life and nourishes us day by day. The language of intimacy is the pathway we desire.

The Bible points the way, often using language that is so bold we hardly dare speak it ourselves. Throughout the Old Testament, metaphors of sexuality are used to describe both God's personality and actions. Often we are unaware of this imagery since we read English translations instead of the original Hebrew and Greek, the result being that the emotional content of some figures of speech as well as their intellectual import are lost to us. Even the English translations, however, introduce us to a God whose very nature includes the qualities which in the human race are differentiated into male and female. The first chapter of Genesis declares that the human race, male and female, was created in God's own image. These verses tremble with mystery, switching back and forth between the known and the unknown, between oneness and differentiation, between sexuality and divinity. Humankind is unified, but at the same time male and female are distinguished from each other. This male and female humanity points us to the image of God. We are left unsure about the import, bewildered concerning the way that our sexual polarity helps us understand the image of God. Even greater is the mystery of how the "image of God" expresses the nature of the transcendent God who stands just beyond the farthest reaches of our sight. What is clear in this passage, as Phyllis Trible points out in her studies of Genesis, is that the complementary duality of humankind is different from animal sexuality and that it points in the direction of the majestic and infinite God.[12]

Knowing this, we are better able to deal with the way that Scripture and Christian tradition talk about God. We are all well acquainted with the bold use of father as a title of God. The psalmist calls out, "Thou art my Father, my God, and the Rock of my salvation" (89:26), and in the later Isaiah the prophet confesses, "Thou, O Lord, art our Father, our Redeemer from of old is thy name" (63:16). Jesus takes up this title and teaches it to his disciples, with the result that in the New Testament, Father is the dominant name given to God; and the Father-Son metaphor is the most frequent way of distinguishing between God transcendent and God incarnate. From that beginning, this term of cautious intimacy has become deeply imprinted in the entire body of Christian prayer and liturgical speech.

We have been less aware of the fact that the biblical religious experience also uses motherly metaphors to express the nature and work of God. Although this other side of the sexual polarity is less obvious, especially in translations, it is a major element in the early tradition of the Judeo-Christian tradition. One word often translated "mercy" appears frequently as a major aspect of God's character. Its root is the word which means womb. Thus every time that the word for the mercy of God was uttered in Hebrew, the womanly dimensions of God were implied. The force of this word can be recognized by reading a few sentences in which it is translated womblove. The great prayer of confession offered by Ezra, when Jerusalem was restored, is one example; it contrasts God's great love and faithfulness and the continuing sin of the people. Ezra states the people's sin in making the golden calf in the wilderness, but then he recites this fact about God:

> But you did not abandon them there in the desert,
>   for your *womblove* is great.
> You did not take away the cloud or the fire
>   that showed them the path by day and night.
> In your goodness you told them what they should do;
>   you fed them manna and gave them water to drink. (Neh. 9:19-20 TEV, altered)

In verses 27, 28, and 31 this same word appears. Psalm 25:6 says this of God: "Be mindful of thy *womblove*, O Lord, and of thy steadfast love, for they have been from of old" (RSV, altered). Isaiah 63:15 is an especially interesting passage: "The yearning of thy heart (digestive organs) and thy *womblove* are withheld from me" (RSV, altered).

In the second part of Isaiah (see 46:3-4 and 66:1-16) and in Jeremiah 31:15-22, the metaphorical language is especially interesting. In Isaiah 46 the language is ambiguous. God bears us; but what is not clear is whether God is the pregnant mother carrying the child in her womb; or is God the expectant father hovering over his wife with eager anxiety? This ambivalence in the metaphor seems fully consistent with the insight expressed in Genesis 1 that God embraces in the divine character both dimensions of humankind, both male and female as we know these qualities in our divided existence.

The use of female imagery for God's character and work is much more extended than these few paragraphs reveal. Summing up her own survey and presentation of the evidence, Trible concludes:

God conceives in the womb; God fashions in the womb; God judges in the womb; God destines in the womb; God brings forth from the womb; God receives out of the womb; and God carries from the womb to gray hairs. From this uterine perspective, then, Yahweh molds life for individuals and for the nation Israel. Accordingly, in biblical traditions an organ unique to the female becomes a vehicle pointing to the compassion of God. [13]

In Christian worship of later times, this recognition of the polarity in God's own nature has dimmed. Much hymnody and prayer have stressed God's fatherliness and split off the motherliness, ascribing this quality to Mary, to Jesus, to the Spirit, or to the saints. God the Father has become more austere, more separated from experience, while the substitutes for the God who bears her children and nurses them at her breasts manifest the intimacy that is basic to the divine personality.

There are two problems with current ways that Christians do call God Father. One is that this word has become a technical term rather than a title expressing intimacy. We use it to identify the first person of the Trinity; thus God the Father is distinguished from God the Son or God the Holy Spirit. Although clarity of reference is appropriate, it is regrettable that so powerful and emotional a word as father has been pressed into this technical and abstract service. The other problem is that father is given such preeminence over other figures of speech. Savior, redeemer, consuming fire, light, love are New Testament terms ascribed to God, but we scarcely notice them, so constant is our use of father as the mode of address.

The broadening of our liturgical language, which this chapter is recommending, therefore, will include a richer use of terms of intimacy. We will continue to use the title Father, but deliberately, when that is what we mean to say, instead of as the verbal ejaculation it now seems to be. At the same time we need to recover in our prayer language the biblical imagery that includes the female pole of humankind as vehicles for the metaphors. [14] At first, these efforts may seem strange to the ear. Many people will start with similes instead of metaphors: "O God, as a mother nurtures her child, so you care for the people whom you bring into the world." Some will link Father and Mother together, as Percy Dearmer does in the hymn where he says of God: "Our father and mother and maker art thou." Or we may prefer a hyphenated term, as Joseph Fort Newton used it: "Father-Mother God. . . ."[15] In time we may find ourselves praying to our heavenly Mother, at first privately, then in small groups, and then in regular services of worship.

Again, Theodore Parker gives us an example. At first, he slipped in references to Mother almost as an afterthought: O Thou Creating and Protecting Power, who art our Father, yea, our Mother not the less, . . ." (p. 22). Later he could give these metaphors equal place: ". . . thou art our Father, and our Mother" and "foldest in thine arms all the worlds which thou hast made, and warmest with thy mother's breath each mote that peoples the sun's beams . . ." (p. 31). Although Parker tended to pair these references, there are times later in the decade covered by the published prayers when God is addressed as Our heavenly Mother without any reference to the Father.

Other terms can also be used to express intimacy with God. *Gates of Prayer* uses the title Blessed One. I am not sure how to describe the vibrations from that term. It is not part of my family life, but if it were it would more likely describe my feelings toward my wife than those toward either my children or my parents. Blessed One suggests reverence that recognizes both the transcendence of God and the imminence of the One who inspired the love lyrics of The Song of Solomon. The Jewish prayers that I have been reading do not draw extensively upon metaphors of family life, but they are filled with the sense of friendship with God, of peace in the presence of the Creator, of joy and love because of the One who cares for us completely. They bless "the Eternal God, who removes sleep from the eyes, slumber from the eyelids," just as countless fathers and mothers and lovers have done through the ages.[16] If we continue to brood upon the language of intimacy and the metaphors it provides, the time may come when we can speak as boldly of God as now we do of Jesus: "Jesus, lover of my soul, / Let me to thy bosom fly." When we reach that point in our piety we will discover that the psalmist long ago had made that same discovery about God (Ps. 131):

O Lord, I am not proud;
I have no haughty looks.

I do not occupy myself with great matters,
or with things that are too hard for me.

But I still my soul and make it quiet,
like a child upon its mother's breast;
my soul is quieted within me.

O Israel, wait upon the Lord,
from this time forth for evermore. [17]

Developing a New Feeling for Language

In this chapter I am proposing a major shift in the idioms of
prayer—a shift away from those we learned long ago and have
practiced constantly since then. These idioms have made deep
grooves in our mental processes so that some verbal patterns sound
right and come naturally into mind and voice. It takes a long time to
relearn the feeling for language. Some of us, for example, have taken
a decade to move from *thee* and *thou* to *you*.

Some of the strangeness we will experience comes from the fact
that we are doing new things; in a little while we will grow
accustomed to new patterns and images, and be able to use them
more easily. In some cases, however, the strangeness will indicate
that the pattern or phrasing doesn't work well. It may be mere
awkwardness or an unnatural use of words. There will be times when
our trials result in prayers that are inappropriate for public
congregational use, or which can be questioned on theological
grounds.

Despite these dangers, most of us will continue to move forward,
carefully, gently, persistently. We can read the prayers that others
write, invite friends to comment on ours, and practice in private. In
personal devotions and in our study time we can compose prayers
using the new idioms. Some of these new compositions can be
published in church newsletters or used in small group meetings;
then they can make their way into the Sunday service.

Many people are involved in this creative venture. New idioms and patterns are on their way, and it is our privilege to share in this creative process.

God of love and kindness, Source of life, all praise is yours.
Long ago you led your people into a land flowing with milk and
*   honey,*
*   and fed them with the bread of life.*
You gave them Jerusalem as a place where they could live in peace
*   and freedom, there giving them your mother's milk of life.*
In these latter days you have provided America as this new land of
*   plenty, this new place where hungry people can find the*
*   nourishment*
*   they need for body and soul.*
Source of life, all praise is yours.

Today, O God, we pray for America, our beloved land—
*   its rivers fouled and its air polluted,*
*   its forests depleted and its farm land ravaged,*
*   its villages decaying and its cities crowded and*
*   festering with injustice,*
*   its people cynical and its leaders baffled by the*
*   immensity of the problems facing us.*

Where we have sinned, forgive us.
Where we have failed to understand, give us wisdom.
Where we have grown weary in our work, give us new strength.
Where we have lost our hope, restore our vision.

God of love and kindness, Source of life, all praise is yours.

Making Room

4

For as the heavens are higher than the earth,
so are my ways higher than your ways
and my thoughts than your thoughts. (Isa. 55:9)

The next step seems so very easy. As our stock of liturgical language grows, we should make room for it by cutting back the traditional and commonplace words and ceremonies. As I work on this challenge, middle-aged father that I am, I find that cutting back is very much like sorting children's books accumulated through the years; both tasks are more difficult than I had expected. Memories come back, long familiar words take on life again, the wisdom of past generations again becomes persuasive.

This recognition about worship struck me with special force on a wintry day in our nation's capital. I was one of one hundred fifty pastors and professors of worship from many churches gathered for worship in a rearranged chapel at Catholic University of America. We had been together for four days discussing our mutual concerns for worship, offering our praises and prayers together, and enjoying one another's friendship. Soon we were to brave the first snow of the season and find our ways back to our separate places of work across North America. The liturgy of the day was the celebration of the Lord's Supper according to the pattern of the Roman Rite of 1969. There were elements that are not of my own tradition—classical eucharistic vestments, the use of incense, and ceremonies like kissing the altar. The music was contemporary and strong, skillfully led by cantors and organist, and sung heartily by this diverse congregation. Everything seemed to fit together, the liturgy, its style, the very catholic quality of the physical space where we were meeting, even the tone of the congregation. There was something immensely satisfying about this event despite the fact that it expressed the tradition of a church greatly different from my own.

The power of a long and coherent piety, framed in emotive ceremonial form, affected my senses and my mind. How could anyone ask that the service be changed when everything seemed so good?

Yet change it will. The metaphors of masculinity were too powerfully present, in the Gloria Patri after psalms and hymns, in the masculine naming of God in the major prayers, in the dominance of males in the leading of the service, all of which was intensified by the patriarchal authority of the tradition which pervaded the assembly.

Let there be no ambiguity or uncertainty: Christian prayer will continue to call God *Father*. As a name of God, this word is an essential aspect of our theological tradition. As a metaphorical vehicle, rooted in one of the most powerful aspects of human life, Father communicates certain insights into the divine character, insights conveyed by no other word. What needs to be changed is not the fact that Christian prayer uses fatherly language, but the way that it is used. In the future this masculine language will be used less frequently and more carefully.

Let there be no ambiguity or uncertainty: Christian prayer in the future will be more diverse than it now is, drawing upon a wide range of figurative language, including metaphors that are inescapably female. Prayer in the biblical, Christian tradition has always been bold in its use of metaphors; and we live in a time when that boldness is especially needed.

These two convictions converge in a third interim principle: *during this transitional period there should be a careful and selective reduction of masculine metaphors in services of worship*. Although this principle can be stated in a more positive way, by saying that masculine metaphors should be used with greater clarity and precision than in the past, I have chosen to stress the negative form of the principle because it puts the challenge to us more directly. At this point in the process of change, the rhythm is necessarily that of expansion and contraction. By using the metaphors of masculinity with less frequency we will create space for the enlarged metaphorical language that is developing out of our study and prayer.

For some time I have been preparing services in which I cut out the unnecessary masculinities—the generic terms, certain masculine metaphors for God, the traditions that assume that leaders of worship ought to be male. My goal has been simple enough—to see whether theologically and liturgically strong services can be created according to this expansion/contraction alternation. My conclusion is that the approach works, at least in those settings where leaders may choose their own materials. It is possible to select psalms and hymns and to offer prayers that are devout, orthodox, and consistent with the divine majesty, yet freed from conventional and unnecessary masculinities of language. These services can still be alive, interesting, and true.[1]

To create such liturgies, however, requires work, sensitivity, and skill. The words of hymns and psalms have to be examined carefully, Scripture studied with new questions and objectives, prayer books evaluated by different criteria, and sermons prepared according to new guidelines. This work sometimes will be solitary—minister or musician working at the task alone. In some settings, the task will be shared by larger groups of people who are committed to the establishing of reformed linguistic usage.

Using the Language of the Psalms

One of the major tests of this expansion/contraction approach is the way we use portions of the Psalms which, along with other biblical lyrics, have long been major expressions of Christian praise. Daily services in churches and monasteries are built around the recitation of the Psalter, and selections of psalmody have punctuated the reading of Scripture in the main Sunday service of most churches. In the Reformed branch of the Protestant tradition only the biblical Psalms could be used as the hymnody for worship. Not until the early 1700s did these forerunners of today's Baptists, Presbyterians, Disciples, and United Church of Christ members ease up on the exclusive use of psalms and accept other kinds of hymns as appropriate elements of divine worship.[2] Even though current use of psalmody is greatly attenuated, restricted mainly to responsive readings and as the source for calls to worship and similar liturgical sentences, the Psalter still continues to be important for Christian worship.

Because of this prominence, we have to respond to problems connected with the fact that many of these biblical lyrics are addressed to the people rather than to God. Even in ancient times some psalms performed functions similar to calls to worship in contemporary worship. Some were instructions for the people's benefit, while others were pastoral exhortations. Psalm 95, which opens the traditional Liturgy of the Hours, illustrates this kind of psalm.[3] The speaker addresses the other worshipers: "O come, let us sing to the Lord," and then explains why (vs. 3-5) by describing God's sovereignty over other gods, over nature, and over history. Because God is being talked about, the narrator uses third-person pronouns, the result being that this psalm is filled with a string of hes and hims.

Other psalms give the same problem—third-person singular pronouns—but for a different reason. Exhibiting an early form of Hebrew prayer, these psalms put the description of God's wonderful acts in a descriptive mode, thus using third-person forms.[4] Other psalms use another pattern in which all of God's actions are "repeated back to God" in the prayer. The descriptive form, using third-person pronouns, expressed a deep sense of deference to the Almighty. Just as we may lower our gaze and step back when meeting a person who commands our love and admiration, so the people who developed these psalms step back from their encounter with God and frame their speech in a deferential third person.

The attitude of submission is not the problem; rather the pronouns are what bother us. Psalm 131, which does not have the third-person pronouns, expresses the submissive mode we all know to be authentic: "O Lord, my heart is not lifted up. . . . But I have calmed and quieted my soul, like a child quieted at its mother's breast." This prayer is suitable for all believers in God.

The conclusion seems inescapable: for the time being, we will ordinarily use psalms which speak directly to God, rather than those that praise God indirectly with third-person language. Much good material is available for our use but we do have to take time to select carefully.

For some time I have been using a table of psalms for Sunday worship as a guide to selecting opening sentences for the service.

Since the table has been prepared for the purpose of using the Psalter extensively, it uses many psalms which refer to God in the third person. I am finding, however, that by selecting verses carefully it often is possible to maintain the "second-person principle." On those occasions when the psalm does not provide this possibility I choose from a different psalm or canticle.

A few psalms are so deeply engrained in the soul of Christian worship that I am ready to use them even though they refer to God in the third person. It is hard to imagine Christian worship without Psalms 23, 24, 100, 121, and 150. One advantage to the expansion/contraction approach to the challenge of language is that we leave ourselves room to use a few third-person psalms without making worship seem heavily male.

Trinitarian Ascriptions of Praise

A second problem connected to the use of the Psalter is the ancient practice of surrounding these Jewish lyrics with a doxology of praise. Again, the problem is not with the basic idea but with the way that we do it. When David brought the ark of the covenant to Jerusalem (I Chron. 15 and 16), he "appointed that thanksgiving be sung to the Lord" (16:7). The musicians responded with excerpts from Psalms 105, 96, and 106, concluding with:

> Blessed be the Lord, the God of Israel,
> from everlasting to everlasting!

In later years Christians have followed this example; but the form of the doxology has been changed. It now specifies the true nature of this God who is being praised: "Glory be to the Father and to the Son and to the Holy Ghost." Psalms, other canticles, and many hymns now are concluded with this brief, trinitarian doxology of praise.

At this point I am tempted to formulate a new liturgical rule: if a formula gets in the way of worshiping God, then drop the formula. For many Protestants this rule can be applied easily to the Gloria following psalms since our hymnal selections have not used the Gloria anyway. Only recently have we learned about the ancient practice of singing this psalm doxology and therefore we can quickly unlearn it. The change may be more difficult for people long accustomed to the formulaic Gloria after psalms. The liturgical function of christening Old Testament lyrics can be accomplished by using psalm prayers, as is illustrated in the *Lutheran Book of Worship*, whose editors state that "the psalm prayer strikes a clearly Christian note, making the Gloria Patri unnecessary."[5] The aesthetics of discontinuing the singing of the Gloria Patri is more difficult to resolve. The rhythm of the words, especially when accompanied by physical movements such as bowing or singing, is not easily replaced. Some worshipers may decide that this particular use of "Glory Be to the Father" is so important that they have to continue it despite their intention to cut back in their use of masculine language.

A similar problem arises because of the custom to pattern hymns after psalms, even though their Christian orientation is clear. Thus, the final stanza of some hymns has become a trinitarian ascription of praise. Because of the strict requirements of meter and rhyme, these doxologies have varied widely. Even so, most of them have explicitly ascribed praise to Father, Son, and Holy Spirit. In some cases this doxological stanza was part of the original poem, but some hymns were composed without this formulaic ending, which was added later, probably to justify the singing of "amen" at the close.[6]

Why sing that final stanza, especially if it was added later? There is no confusion about the nature of God that requires this constant repetition of the formulaic words. Nor is the praise of God threatened by leaving them out, since that function properly belongs to the text of the hymn and the intentions of the singers. The doxology at the close is usually not necessary for theological reasons.

Of course, liturgical orthodoxy has insisted on the importance of singing all verses without omission so that we would get the full intention of the writer. Even if the hymnal editors have given us all verses of the original, which often is not the case, this policy is based on a misunderstanding of the nature of congregational song. The words are joined with a tune to make a new vehicle for transmitting the souls of the singers to God. Continuity and fullness of text are not the primary considerations. Some final verses may be so important to the meaning and movement of a hymn that they cannot be omitted. If they are strong and if the people know them well, they probably can be continued. After all, this interim principle calls only for reduction of masculinities, not for elimination of all of them.

In many Protestant churches the Gloria Patri and the doxology are the two liturgical songs known by the congregations. At certain times in worship, a chord on the piano or organ will bring the people to their feet to sing. These two acclamations have always needed rest for periods of time so that the tunes would not be abused by overuse. Now, a new reason can be added for developing additional ways of praising "God in three persons, blessed Trinity."

One way of doing so is to draw on the appropriate verses of some hymns, especially some already well known to the congregations. "Holy, Holy, Holy! Lord God Almighty" (which is sung, with a nice sense of appropriateness, to the tune "Nicaea") has two verses which could be used, each beginning with the "holy" ascription and ending with the phrase "God in three Persons, blessed Trinity." (Note that the editors of the *Lutheran Book of Worship* have altered "tho' the eye of sinful man" in verse three to read "though the eye made blind by sin.") The final stanza of "Come, Thou Almighty King" also proclaims the praise of the trinitarian God. Following the lead of the *Lutheran Book of Worship*, one pronoun is changed from the deferential third person to the direct second person, which is consistent with the rest of the hymn:

> To thee, great One in Three,
> Eternal praises be,
> Hence, evermore:
> Thy sovereign majesty
> May we in glory see,
> And to eternity
> Love and adore!

Another act of praise with clear emphasis upon creator and redeemer is an Isaac Watts text which can be sung very nicely to the tune "Old Hundredth."

From all that dwell below the skies,
Let the Creator's praise arise;
Let the Redeemer's name be sung,
Through every land by every tongue.

Eternal are thy mercies, Lord;
Eternal truth attends thy word:
Thy praise shall sound from shore to shore,
Till suns shall rise and set no more.

Other hymn segments can also be used as the instrument of congregational praise. Usually one such doxology will be used over a period of weeks and perhaps months, the text printed in the bulletin until the congregation no longer is dependent on the printed text.

Hymns Old and New

In a general assembly of my own church body, the worship services featured hymns written during the past three decades, many of them published by the Hymn Society. While the intention was commendable, the results were unsatisfactory because the language was often trite and too frequently depended on language now considered sexist. On the spot, I created another Watkins interim rule: if the hymn text was recently composed, is unfamiliar to congregations, and problematic, discard it; nothing is to be gained by trying to repair a liturgical lemon.

The discarding of a hymn is more difficult when the text is well known, much loved, and often sung. Even after leaving out a problematic verse, some hymns are difficult because the major poetic form depends on masculine imagery. How does the interim principle of selective reduction work in these instances?

For the time being, some hymns may have to be set aside because the problems are so severe. Several times I have sat in the seminary chapel working through Gerhard Tersteegen's magnificent hymn of praise, wondering how it could be made more serviceable. Its structure resists change: "God *himself* is present; . . . *Him* alone, God we own,

Him, our God and Savior; Praise *his* name forever!" Here masculine pronouns are put forward aggressively and the grammatical structure is used to convey the intensity of this act of praise. Perhaps a new translation could be developed; but as it now stands in the books, this hymn may have to be momentarily retired. "He Leadeth Me" is another hymn that needs to be set aside because it needlessly aggravates the language problem, routinely substituting he for God. Some hymns are so troublesome in their people language that they too require discontinuation. Even Whittier's name can no longer justify "O brother man, fold to thy heart thy brother."

The loss of some commonly sung hymns may not be so great a disaster for, as Erik Routley points out, the greatest offenders of the inclusive language principles are hymns by British and American writers between 1850 and 1950. Rather than hymns "about the glory of God, the beauty of Christ, and the delights of heaven," themes of the classical hymns, these later hymns exhort us to social justice and love for one another. Although justice and love need to be retained in the vocabulary of worship, the language does have to be chosen carefully.[7] So too in hymnody and worship.

A great many hymns, although largely satisfactory with respect to masculinity of language, do have one or two problematic words or phrases. To eliminate these hymns right now would decimate our liturgies and impoverish our religious experience. Therefore, despite blemishes, some of these hymns can continue to be used if we are careful in our management of the process. Most people can handle one such hymn in a service, especially if the tune and text are strong and well known. For example, although "O Worship the King" begins with verses cast in the he-mode, it later switches to the you-mode. Its imagery is strong and in most cases not dependent on sexual metaphors. The people-talk is suitable. My vote would be to continue using this hymn, trying to balance it in services with other hymns that do not use the he-mode of addressing God.

Some people try to deal with these slight blemishes by suggesting that words be changed, either printing the alternatives in the bulletin or announcing them orally. The advantage of this practice is that it quickly fixes the troublesome word or phrase and shows that the sympathies of the leaders favor the broadening of liturgical language. The disadvantages are that these changes sometimes generate controversy that is more detrimental to the human spirit than the damage done by unreconstructed hymns. These changes may also barbarize the text of the hymn, a serious problem since worship is too often squalid even now. Because this kind of change is made locally, each congregation develops its own form of hymns, thus making it more difficult for Christian unity to be experienced.

My conclusion is that the main responsibility for altering texts is lodged with hymnal editors who, it can be hoped, possess the skill to make deft and suitable alterations. Because their revisions are widely disseminated, the work of these editors is less likely to splinter the liturgical consensus and the body of Christ. We can rejoice that hymnal committees are moving forward in this task of revising standard hymn texts. Already their labors have borne fruit in the hymnal portion of the *Lutheran Book of Worship*.

During this interim period, however, most ministers and musicians have to deal with unrevised hymnals. Once purchased, a set of these books will last twenty years or more. Even some recently edited books are still sexist through and through. The problem is illustrated by the situation in one congregation where I conducted an *ad interim* Sunday ministry for several months. Their hymnal was edited in the late seventies, newly purchased prior to my coming, and duly supplied with memorial bookplates. Its language for people and God is unreconstructed. What are ministers and musicians to do?

The first step is a comprehensive analysis of the complete book. Every hymn, reading, and prayer should be read through, felt-tip marker in hand, every difficult word or phrase highlighted in the desk copy. In this way the book will be learned and the extent of the challenge made evident. By marking the problematic elements, worship planners will be able in the future to recognize quickly the problems they need to consider.

The analysis can then proceed to a second step which is to make lists. One group of entries will include hymns and readings that are fully acceptable with respect to language; and another group will be made up of items that seem unusable during this interim period. A third list will include items that can be used by selecting stanzas or items where blemishes are slight and the hymn or reading can be managed without change. A fourth list could indicate items which are severely blemished but which nevertheless might be usable under specialized circumstances.

I am assuming every hymnal will be serviceable part of the time. The need to supplement hymnals does have to be faced. Most worship leaders have gone beyond their hymnal once in a while for other reasons than language, especially for the purpose of using a hymn with seasonal references or theological emphases. Many song leaders have supplemented the standard hymnal with an occasional gospel song. The practice of supplementing is not new.

One way of adding to the hymnal is to purchase a supplementary collection of hymns. One example is *Creation Sings*, a booklet of fifty-five hymns chosen, says the compiler, "so that they may be sung by any individual or group without provoking conscious or unconscious sexual distinctions or ranking of any kind."[8] Some hymns in this collection are new compositions which rise up to the new standards of inclusiveness. Others are adapted slightly. Some of the older texts, however, still use masculine pronouns for God and the title Father in doxological verses. Yet this collection and others like it may be the interim solution for some congregations with especially troublesome hymnals.

Another way of supplementing is to produce one's own congregational supplement, using in it the hymns chosen because they exemplify the principles to which ministers and musicians, as well as worship committees, are committed.

Whenever we reproduce, however, we face a new set of ethical and legal issues. Hymn texts and tunes are artistic creations protected by law. Engravings and type set in books are under the control of those who publish them. The fact that we can reproduce so easily and usually not get caught in no way frees us from the moral obligation of respecting the just claims controlled by copyright laws.

In the process of evaluating, adapting, and supplementing hymnals, broader questions of pastoral leadership are involved. These are topics which I will address in later chapters.

Speech Patterns in Sermons and Other Oral Usage

An especially difficult challenge is to reduce masculinity in our normal speech patterns, two of which need to be discussed here. One is primarily found in people-talk when we phrase statements in the singular: "A minister . . . he. . . ." The other pattern uses pronouns to reduce the number of times that it is necessary to repeat nouns. Both patterns tend to fill our speech unnecessarily with masculine forms. Once we become aware of what we are saying, it is possible to begin making changes in the way we construct our sentences and express our ideas.

It takes more than awareness. Even new books are being published in which authors admit the problem and then excuse themselves from dealing with it. One author I have been reading, for example, justified the use of masculine singular formulations by saying that in the past theologians have usually been men. If this author's only reference to theologians were to them in the past tense, then this self-defense has some justification. Yet this writer uses the same pattern in passages that deal with theologians today. Here the failure to alter sentence structure is neither justified nor justifiable. Our language can no longer be spoken or written this way.

One of the simplest devices in people-talk is to put certain general nouns in the plural rather than in the singular, with the result that the pronoun is the plural *they* rather than the singular *he, she,* or *it.* Why say, "A preacher should avoid gratuitous masculine references in *his* sermon"? It is a little better to say: "A preacher should avoid gratuitous masculine references in *his or her* sermon." (Surely we can agree that the slash technique is to be condemned; either form [she/he, s/he] is unpronounceable and scrapes like nails on glass.) Why not say, "Preachers should avoid gratuitous masculine references in *their* sermons"? This theory is simple; but for some reason it is difficult to put into practice. At least my speech patterns are resistant; even after three years of determined effort, I still find myself falling into the singular noun, he-or-she-pronoun routine. Once the sentence begins in the singular, the speaker is (I've done it again). What I should be saying is: When sentences begin in the singular, speakers are trapped and have to wriggle out with as much grace as possible.

More difficult to resolve is the pronoun problem when the referent is God who has ordinarily been referred to in liturgical language in masculine gender. Since we always think and speak of God in the singular, even when we use trinitarian formulas, we cannot adopt the simple expedient of recasting sentences in plural forms. We can discontinue all of these third-person pronouns, using the name God every time the pronoun appears. Even *himself* would be changed to Godself.[9] I have used this device on a very limited basis when reading from the Psalter in worship. There are places, in fact, when the congregation's ability to understand the passage is strengthened when *he* is replaced by *God* or *the Lord*. While this practice reduces the masculinity of speech about God, it has two limiting characteristics. The frequent repetition of this one word is jarring to the ear. Its very crudeness becomes a problem. The second difficulty is more serious. By greatly increasing the frequency of usage, we give this term a weight that can be questioned.

A second technique is to rearrange sentences so that we use adjectives and epithets in some of the places where we have previously used pronouns. Many sentences use God as the significant noun, followed by another phrase or clause that is dependent on God in meaning and grammar. "In Genesis it says that God created human beings in his own image." Or, ". . . in the hope that they too will come to know God and to live the new life that *he* gives." In both of these examples, the pronouns could be changed into *God* or *God's*. The advantage is that absolute precision is retained, since there can be no doubt whose image it is and who does the giving. Both sentences could also be revised by other means. The adjectival approach would change the pronoun in the first sentence fragment to divine—". . . that God created human beings in the divine image"; and in the second sentence to the phrase

God-given—". . . to know God and to live that new God-given
life." Often one of the uses of the divine name or the relative
pronoun can be replaced by epithets which clearly refer to God.
When the context makes it clear that God and the one described by
the epithet are the same person, and when the texture of the sentence
permits, phrases such as "the Holy One" (or Eternal, Infinite,
All-wise) can be used.

This deliberate recasting of prose style is a demanding intellectual
activity. In conversation and in extempore speaking such as
sermons, the challenge is even greater because there is no chance to
cross out a poor start. Our goal should be to speak about God in ways
that are always clear, always graceful, always faithful to the divine
nature as it has been revealed to us.

Much as I love my mother tongue, I do not believe that its syntax is
divinely inspired. Some of its current patterns of usage make us say
things we do not want to say, placing upon us the obligation to find
different patterns that do accomplish our intentions. It takes time,
but if the challenge is understood to be as much linguistic and
intellectual as it is religious, we are more likely to rise to it with zest
and good humor—and godly zeal.

Holy One of Israel:
We stand awestruck by your blazing glory,
your magnificent and creative power,
your faithful and steadfast love,
your just and merciful guidance of the whole world.

How can we help but honor you because of the excellency of your
       character?
How can we help but love you for your own self,
    warm, complex, challenging, and ever present in all life's
       experiences?

Holy One of Israel, the great I Am of everything that is,
    we praise your holy Name.

Memory and Hope

5

Let us offer to God acceptable worship,
with reverence and awe;
for our God is a consuming fire. (Heb. 12:28b-29)

The language of prayer is but part of a much larger reality, religious faith itself. What we say in our liturgical assemblies is directly connected to the combination of belief and action that constitutes our religion. This connection is true whether the religion is an ancient patriarchal faith such as Judaism and Christianity, or a new feminist faith such as veneration of the Great Goddess.[1] Previous chapters have dealt lightly with this connection since the expansion/contraction procedure avoids awkward aspects of the tradition and works at developing new dimensions. The unexpressed presupposition is that this revision of liturgical language constitutes reform that is fully consistent with the nature of the faith itself. Certainly, the expansion/contraction methodology makes it possible to sidestep in public much of the difficulty with the patriarchal dimension of the Judeo-Christian tradition.

Footwork, however, works only part of the time. The patriarchal character is central to the received tradition, and regular liturgical life brings us directly into contact with that fact. The Bible—which all of us have to read in services of worship—and several of the most hallowed liturgical formularies such as the Lord's Prayer are explicitly and predominantly male in their language. No amount of expansion and contraction will change that fact. I can understand why some people have abandoned the traditions of the church. If we take its language seriously, we have to do something—yield, leave, or develop some other way of dealing with the intractable maleness of its books, formularies, and patterns of leadership.

Obviously, I'm staying with the church. It's easy to do because the tradition supports my personhood and gives me a place to work. Besides, I have been shaped for nearly half a century by its systems and symbols. For me, the church as a community of memory is the source of life and livelihood. Other people, especially younger women, are also staying but they depend less upon the past than upon the future. Remembering that a community is shaped as much by its hope as by its memory, these people emphasize the prophetic character of the Judeo-Christian tradition. They point to a time still to come when we will experience a broadened, transformed, and more complete version of the Christian faith.

That time has not yet come and meanwhile we have to plan worship for next Sunday, which means reading from the Bible and saying the creed as well as offering prayer. Another interim principle can guide us: *during this transitional period, we will continue to read the Bible and offer certain prayers even though their phrasing depends so much on the metaphors of masculinity; our sermons and other liturgical comments will provide the contemporary corrective.*

The Public Reading of the Bible

Built upon the foundations of Judaism, Christianity is a religion of a Book. Through the generations that Book has been dissected and analyzed, explained and defended, mistreated and honored. These varied uses have been based on the fact that virtually every branch and blossom of the church has accepted the Bible as objective reality that has to be dealt with. It is there to be studied in private, read and preached in worship, and systematically expounded in classrooms and lecture halls. Our meditations, liturgies, and theologies move far beyond Scripture; but they always start there.

This unyielding commitment to the Bible continues despite the fact that it is so archaic a book. Even with all their learning, scholars still have not discovered the secrets of its origins in ancient Israel and not quite so ancient Christianity. Whether Moses or nameless redactors are responsible for the Pentateuch, these writings come from a culture greatly different from our own—with thought patterns, social customs, public institutions, and political structures that are alien to ours. Because of our common humanity, we can understand their passions and ideas despite the distance between us. Yet our worlds are different.

This alien character of Scripture is expressed, in part, by the difference in language and thought forms. Hebrew and Greek from antiquity are greatly different from idiomatic English in the late twentieth century. Even when well translated, many passages use ideas and phrases that depend upon a world view that we do not share. Frequently, the Bible assumes or supports social customs we no longer understand or approve.

The conflict between our commitment to the Bible and our commitment to a new expression of inclusiveness is renewed every time the church gathers for worship. Week after week we read the Bible in a ceremony that calls attention to the importance of this book. Our choices of the passages to be read are guided by liturgical traditions, especially the lectionary that appoints certain readings for each Sunday of the year.[2] Because the theory back of the lectionary stresses the value of transcending the interests and convictions of pastors, we are kept from selecting only the passages that are free from masculine metaphors and linguistic use. Consequently, we will regularly encounter awkward passages. In the season of Advent (cycle A of the ecumenical lectionary) eight of the twelve lections, according to the Revised Standard Version, have some problem with respect to language. It may be only a single use of a masculine pronoun for God; or the problem may be more severe. All four Sundays present difficulties in at least one of the readings.

We cannot deal with the problem by rewriting the Bible. What is written is written, and one source of its value is that it remains the same generation after generation. Thomas Aquinas, Martin Luther, Teresa of Avila, Jonathan Edwards, and Karl Barth all worked with the same set of writings as we do. This emphasis on the integrity of the text also makes me hostile toward certain paraphrases in widespread use. When we cut ourselves adrift from the objective fact of the biblical text, we simultaneously cut ourselves adrift from one source of unity and from one anchor against being "tossed to and fro and carried about with every wind of doctrine" (Eph. 4:14).

This objectivity of the text, however, holds true for the Bible in its original languages. Some of the problems encountered today do not exist in the original but rather are created by the process of recasting the message from one language to another, a fact which even a casual comparison of reputable translations illustrates. The variations in translations are present because the science is itself so complex. Should translations be literal or dynamic? Should they concentrate upon reproducing the form of the original text or upon the meaning? How do we approximate in English the meaning of grammatical constructions that are greatly different in structure from the way our language is shaped? How can we deal with the changing norms of English and at the same time keep faith with previous generations and the ways they used the language? How can we translate so that the English version can continue to be used in the future?[3]

It makes sense to select the translation that comes closest to being inclusive both in spirit and in accomplishment. At this time, however, there is no single translation to be fully relied on with respect to inclusive language since there always is a time lag between the formation of idiomatic speech and the process of translating. With respect to the generic uses of masculine forms, the lag still exists. Most translators, including those in the past decade, could still assume that man can be used to mean a human being or the human race. They have assumed that masculine singular pronouns can be used when the reference is to a person whose identity or sex is not specified. As a result of this time lag, most translations use some phrasing that now is known to be limiting.

These difficulties are illustrated in an important passage from the writings of Paul, Romans 5:6-19, where the apostle discusses the parallels between Adam and Christ. Each is a representative of the human race, the one bringing sin and death, the other bringing grace and life. In the Revised Standard Version man or men appears twelve times, making this passage sound heavily masculine. In some of these uses the word specifically refers to Adam or Jesus, each of whom is identified in Scripture as a male human being. Yet the Greek text uses a word for man in only four of these twelve

constructions. In the other constructions the Greek text uses one of
the following forms: *tis* which means a certain one when the writer
will not speak more definitely; *enas* whose literal meaning is one;
pantes a word that means all; and an adjective without a noun, with
an ending that is either masculine or neuter. Furthermore, the four
occurrences of the word man use the Greek *anthropos*, a word that
stresses the meaning of human being or person. Not used at all is the
word *aner* which stresses the meaning of adult male. The American
Standard Version of 1901, striving always for a literal translation,
translates man in six of these twelve contructions. Today's English
Version starts off well: "It is a difficult thing for someone to die for a
righteous person. It may be that someone might even dare to die for a
good person" (Rom. 5:7). Later in the passage, however, TEV also
depends upon the English words man and men to translate Greek
constructions that do not include these words. By the time they have
completed the passage the TEV translaters have, regrettably, used
man or men eleven times even though the Greek text uses these
words only four times.

It is to be regretted that so many pastors no longer can use the
original languages in order to compare translations with the Hebrew
and Greek texts and make their own decisions with respect to difficult
passages. How good it would be if a former pastoral practice could be
revived, of preparing one's own translation of the sermon text week
by week; but that wish is perhaps too unrealistic even to dream of.
Since most pastors cannot use the original languages, we are forced
to rely even more upon clues and hints that come from comparing
translations and from careful examination of commentaries and
word books. Analytical reference works, that deal with the structure
of the Hebrew and Greek texts, are of great help.[4]

This pastoral effort to deal seriously with the biblical text will
usually be approved by the people of the congregation if they know
that their pastors are giving themselves so vigorously to the study of
Scripture. Sermons should not become exercises in linguistic
analysis; yet the hard work of being faithful to the text can help
everyone, including people who use suspect paraphrases, to
understand the issues at stake when they claim to stand upon biblical

authority. The effort can be shared with members of the congregation, both in the work of preparing for the worship service and as part of the congregation's educational program.

After we have established a responsible English version of the scripture lessons, we may be able to deal with some of the gender problems by the way we edit them for reading. We have control over where to begin and end the reading and whether to read the entire passage or excerpts. In some lections, the difficult phrase is an apposition or aside that is not germane to the major idea and can be omitted in the reading. The practice of internal editing must be followed with great discretion, however, since the integrity of Scripture is always threatened by the way we pick and choose. Furthermore, ministers invite trouble when they "tamper" with Scripture because of a controversial topic. I learned this on a Sunday early in my ministry when the passage to be read contained a cryptic reference to hell. I omitted it during the public reading because a prospective member whom I knew to have a very sensitive opinion about this matter was attending the service and I didn't want to cause him unnecessary trouble his very first Sunday. But some of my members who already were nervous about the adequacy of my theology were following the reading in their own Bibles and were furious about what I had done. What they argued then, I am inclined to affirm now, that the Scripture stands whatever problems it may cause us. Thus, judicious editing may on some occasions provide relief, but it is not the major remedy for the problem of the patriarchal character of biblical texts.

What may be the best way of handling these readings, with their patriarchal presuppositions, is to read them as they are—but then to use introductions to the readings and sermons as the counterbalance. It is appropriate to bridge the chasm between the ancient world and our own by a paragraph that is carefully composed to introduce the reading for the day. The use of such a paragraph is usually necessary to help the congregation understand the passages which often begin in the middle of the action or part way through the exposition of ideas. Since two or three passages from as many biblical books will usually be read, it is all the more necessary to help people take hold of the readings. Sometimes this explanatory introduction is written out in the worship folder; sometimes it is stated orally by the worship leader. In either case, it provides a way of explaining that the passages in question apply to everyone even though they are written in ways that seem to exclude women and children. These introductions must be brief, a paragraph of three or four sentences is all that can be tolerated; and half a dozen lines of print is probably the maximum that will be read. Carefully prepared and used, this type of contemporary word can provide an effective interpretation of Scripture.

The more extended version of the contemporary word is the sermon which has as one of its purposes the portraying of how the God whose actions are described in the biblical texts continues to act today. It is always to be hoped that the congregation will then be inspired to respond in loving obedience and joyful service. Sermons originate in big bangs, to borrow a phrase from popular science, out of collisions between ancient texts and contemporary experiences. If one or the other element is missing, the religious talk may be useful but it falls short of being a sermon.

Sermons provide the setting for conversation with the first recorders of God's self-revelation. Because preachers represent life in their own time, with its own presuppositions, questions, convictions, and experiences of the divine, they have much to say when they discuss disarmament with Isaiah (Isa. 2:4) or marriage with Paul (I Cor. 7). Part of that conversation with the people long ago is the effort to figure out what they meant and how it translates into life in our own time. What value is there for us in Paul's instructions about using meat sacrificed to idols (I Cor. 10)? Is that chapter to be used primarily as a description of a problem in pagan societies or does it have universal meaning for people in every time and place? What about Paul's use of the word man in Galatians 5 and 6? When does he mean adult male and when a human being? Sometimes we can't decide, no matter how hard we press the discussion, yet even in these cases the congregation is helped by the conversation itself.

Sermons have another, more dynamic function than merely commenting on the form of the text. They become a prophetic word for our time, cutting through our conventional ideas and patterns of

behavior with God's judgment and with the commission to build a
new society of peace and justice. Sometimes this function can be
fostered by subtle means. The gospel reading for Advent I (cycle A) is
Matthew 24:37-44, which urges Christians to be ready for Christ's
return at an hour we do not expect. Two illustrations are given, two
men working in a field and two women grinding at a mill (24:40-41).
By the simple device of choosing the second illustration rather than
the first, preachers can let the sermon begin the movement toward a
new awareness of the place of women in God's coming order. A
more dramatic illustration of this same process is the contrast
between two illustrations in Luke 15 (one of the lections for
September in cycle C). In verses 3-7, the central figure is a man who
loses a sheep, whereas in verses 8-10 it is a woman who loses a coin.
God is compared both to the man and to the woman. Although
preachers have often used the male illustration of God, a significant
shift in the tone of the sermon—although not in the content of the
gospel—will take place if the woman is used as the illustration of
God's persistent love. I wish that I had been sensitive enough to
realize this possibility myself, but such was not the case. The idea
was given to me by a pastor whom I have known for a long time but
who had always seemed to me to be a conservative man. He was in a
group of ministers with whom I was talking about inclusive language
in worship. During the discussion period he volunteered his
experience in text selection so as to take the woman's point of view.
He strongly repeated that the message of the gospel remains the same
but that the tone is certainly transformed.

If we take the biblical message with the seriousness it deserves,
there will be another dimension to our preaching that is more openly
prophetic. One of the dominant characteristics of the biblical
text—especially in the first six books, in the prophetic writings, and
in the New Testament—is its championing of the cause of the poor
and oppressed people. During much of the period covered by the
Old Testament narrative, the Jewish people were in that condition,
and Christians were similarly an oppressed people during the time
described in the New Testament. Most of us who preach enjoy a
comfortable life, with reasonably assured incomes, positions of

honor and perhaps influence. We are free to make decisions and to carry them out. Since most of us who preach are white and male, we can only partially understand the situation of the large number of Americans who are not favored by society. Yet the people are there—often suffering from prejudicial treatment and frequently from oppression. Racial minorities are in this condition. Many older people are acquainted with the facts of growing old and becoming poor. And women have suffered from many of the same prejudicial conditions . . . denial of employment equal to their abilities, unequal legal power, economic discrimination, and a process of socialization that has taught them that such conditions are God's will and therefore to be accepted gratefully and obediently.

Preachers who are true to the Bible will regularly be assigned texts that express God's solidarity with the oppressed. Such texts should be used. The gospel imperative should be proclaimed. And illustrations from contemporary life should be chosen—from the experiences of the minorities of our land, from the conditions experienced by the aging, and from the continuing situation of many women. This kind of preaching will show that the patriarchal form of biblical religion is like the hard shell of an acorn or walnut. It protects the power of new life that will split open the shell, when the season is right, and produce a new and powerful tree.

Before turning to other necessary uses of male metaphors in the liturgy, I want to note that preaching needs to be directed toward them too. It is not desirable, for example, to preface the reciting of the Lord's Prayer with a commentary about the meaning of that title; this interpretation has to be done some other time. It could be a sermon in the regular Sunday service. It might be a sermon prior to baptism, or in the teaching delivered prior to Christian baptism. Similarly other uses of Father in worship, to which we next turn, can be discussed in the ongoing teaching ministry of a congregation.

Necessary Uses of the Title Father

In addition to the Bible readings, certain other liturgical units are irreducibly masculine in their metaphorical base and will continue to be used in worship. My list includes the Lord's Prayer, the Apostles' and Nicene Creeds, and the words spoken at baptism.[5] What is so troubling about these elements is that they are virtually indispensable aspects of our worship, which means that flexibility in liturgical use is hampered by their intractability. To insist that these basic elements of the liturgy must use fatherly language implies that Father is a truer name for God than are other ways suggested by the extended metaphorical base I have recommended earlier. Even while recognizing this problem, I believe that these units will be continued in public worship for years to come.

One reason for retaining Father in the Lord's Prayer is that this form of words is itself biblical. Thus, the antiquity of this formulary means that we have little choice over its content. Our faithfulness to the biblical text mandates that we retain this title for the divine.

Another reason for retaining the Lord's Prayer in its ancient form is that it reveals the piety and theology of the "author of our salvation." There is no question but that *Father* was the most vivid expression of Jesus' experience of God. By using this prayer, we are identified with Jesus' own life, and therefore with Jesus' way of experiencing the Holy One of Israel. Because Jesus is the fountain from whence our faith flows, I see no way around this continuation in Christian worship of a certain priority of Father as the significant family title for God.[6]

How often and in which services will the Lord's Prayer be used? Judging by the format of some service books, it is fitted into most services, including funerals and weddings, and the several services to mark the hours of the day. In this way every liturgical assembly is united to Jesus' own life of devotion to God; and there always is at least one part of the service that everyone knows well enough to recite from memory. In some churches the prayer is used less frequently; ordinarily it is not included in occasional services such as funerals but is retained for use in the regular Sunday liturgy and group devotions, especially when the groups do not have worship books or bulletins.

The fact is that no other prayer can function in the same way. It connects us to Jesus' own life more tightly than does any other prayer. The words whereby he explained the Last Supper with his disciples on the night of his betrayal are perhaps closer to the mystery of our salvation, and thus are absolutely unique in their capacity to reveal God's redeeming love and to generate the renewing of its experienced presence. The prayer he taught his disciples is almost as effective because it reveals the distinctiveness of Jesus' piety, the closeness of his relationship to God, and the comprehensiveness of his vision for human life in this world and the next. If Father is ever to be a name of God voiced in Christian worship, then it will be when the faithful children of God recite the prayer which Jesus taught his brothers and sisters.

The ancient creeds have long been major elements in Christian worship where they have performed several liturgical functions. They have been used as prose poems to praise God, as the language for affirmations of faith, as signs of authentic faith, as responses to preaching, and as ways of contributing to the festival elaboration of services. Although neither creed is found in Scripture, their contents and terms are venerable and unchangeable. We can from time to time prepare new translations but the basic substance of these creeds really cannot be altered. Either we must use them as they have been handed down to us or we must set them aside as we do some prayers and hymns from earlier times.

It is important that Christian worship continually reaffirm the central affirmations of our faith, a function which regular recitation of the creeds has been used to accomplish. Yet this method is very limited in its effectiveness. The creeds have not been used in the churches where I have been member and minister. Even though I understand what creeds are supposed to be, I find it difficult to use them, and this experience is true for members of other church bodies. If the disciplines of one's church permit, the creeds could simply be retired from use on most occasions.

Perhaps we could follow the lead of the synagogue and develop a form of confession that more clearly accomplishes this praise/response function. Jesus' rephrasing of the Shema (see Mark 12:29-31) could be used for this function:

> Jesus answered, "The first commandment is this:
> 'Hear, O Israel: the Lord your God is the only Lord;
> love the Lord your God with all your heart, with all
> your soul, with all your mind, and with all your strength.'
> The second is this: 'Love your neighbour as yourself.'
> There is no other commandment greater than these."
> (Mark 12:29-31 NEB, altered)

By reciting this text, we make clear our membership in Abraham's family, while also signaling our specific membership in the Christian branch of that family. This text is already familiar because in some eucharistic liturgies it has been used as a brief and vigorous introduction to the act of penitence. We can add to this Christian Shema other texts of scripture that develop implications of this basic affirmation. Excerpts from Romans 8 affirm the victory over all powers of heaven and earth which God will give the faithful. Isaiah 42:5-8a renews the terms of the covenant made with the people whom God has called. Colossians 3:12-15 describes qualities of life that are suitable for those who answer this call to love God and neighbor. Romans 12:1-2 can be adapted for use with the Shema, calling upon worshipers to yield themselves to God.

Admittedly, nothing developed now for Christian use can ever duplicate the centrality of the Shema in Jewish worship. Even the creeds and the Lord's Prayer fall short of the universality that *Hear, O Israel* has in the worship of the synagogue. The reason for proposing the Christian Shema is so that an alternative is available in churches that find the creeds inappropriate. This augmented *summary of the law* provides a way of affirming our faith and responding to God's call that is both faithful to our tradition and responsive to our current experiences of the forms of that call.

It should be noted that the summarizing of the faith has also been expressed by certain prayers, especially the eucharistic prayer. By this Great Thanksgiving the congregation gives thanks to God by reciting all that God has done for them in the economy of salvation; and concludes the prayer by renewing their baptismal vows of faithful, joyful obedience. The more our prayers become declarations of praise-filled obedience, the less need we have of the ancient creeds.

This declarative character of the eucharistic prayer is one reason why the title Father has been used so consistently in this prayer, the traditional form of which has been trinitarian, offering our praise-filled thanksgiving for the threefold work of salvation. This prayer has offered thanks for the steadfast love of the one identified as "holy Father, almighty, everlasting God," a love made known in creation and in the history of Israel. Then the prayer has described the saving actions of the life, ministry, death, and resurrection of God's only Son, Jesus Christ. The concluding section has called upon God's Holy Spirit to indwell this action at the table so that the congregation, receiving Christ's body and blood, may be made one body with him. Because the Christian understanding of God, in its definitive form, has used Father and Son as the basic metaphor, this same terminology has been included in the prayer. Not only does this metaphor state a relationship between these two persons of the deity, but it also portrays the texture of the relationship between God and the people whom Christ has saved.

Although there is strong theological and liturgical support for this trinitarian structuring of the eucharistic prayer, the practice is not absolutely binding. The prayer is indeed a prayer, not a systematic theological statement. Its language, therefore, must be chosen carefully but with a degree of flexibility that statements of belief do not tolerate. Prayer is the growing edge of theological language whereas dogma is its conserving anchor. The trinitarian outline can be preserved even if other titles of God are used. Instead of Father, the prayer can use titles and descriptions that express the eternity, infinity, and sovereignty of our God. Jesus' deity can be invoked by terms such as wisdom and word, as well as by savior and redeemer. The Holy Spirit can continue to be described in customary ways since the primary trinitarian formula has not described the relation of the Spirit to the other persons of the Godhead. The new books of worship, however, make it clear that Father will appear in most eucharistic prayers. Even if the title is not used in the main salutation, as in Eucharistic Prayer C of *The Book of Common*

Prayer (1977), it appears later, immediately after the "Holy, holy, holy . . ." hymn of praise. On occasions when church discipline and pastoral factors mandate the use of a prescribed prayer, the Father metaphor will appear. There will be times, however, when leaders of the service are free to adapt the text or to offer the prayer extemporaneously. On these occasions they can broaden the metaphorical base of their prayer language.

The trinitarian formula in Christian baptism presents a different challenge. In the church's earliest period people were baptized "in the name of Jesus Christ" (Acts 2:38; 10:48). Early, however, a fuller statement of faith, from which the Apostles' Creed was probably derived, became normal, and throughout most of Christian history the words said at baptism have included classical trinitarian language: "I baptize you, *name*, in the name of the Father, and of the Son, and of the Holy Spirit." The weight of tradition itself exercises powerful inertial drag, making it difficult to change our practice. A second factor complicates the matter even more. One highly desirable goal is that our membership in the one Body of Christ be recognized, however divided the church may be in its historical life. Lutherans, Disciples, Pentecostals, and Catholics are all to be accepted as Christians because we have all been baptized. When baptism is understood to include both water and the invocation of the Holy Trinity, its authenticity has a good chance of being recognized everywhere. The more our practice modifies the classical pattern, however, the greater is the possibility of renewed contention over a sacrament that is supposed to unite us into the one Body of Christ.

Some efforts have been made to retain the trinitarian form but to change the titles. In its exploratory texts concerning rites of incorporation into the church, the Consultation on Church Union has proposed a possibility. In a service called "An Affirmation of the Baptismal Covenant," intended to be used on occasions when people seek to affirm and claim for themselves what was said at their baptism, four ways of affirming the faith are provided. One of them asks these three questions: "Do you believe in God the Creator, who has made you and all the world? Do you believe in God the Savior, who has redeemed you and all humanity? Do you believe in God the Holy Spirit, who sanctifies you and all the people of God?" Clearly, this affirmation of faith is given a trinitarian structure; it distinguishes between functions of the persons of the Godhead, although it suggests a profound unity that some might argue diminishes the distinctiveness of the three persons of the Trinity. It is significant that this formula comes as the affirmation of baptismal vows rather than as the vows themselves. They stand, therefore, as a commentary upon the traditional formulary, a further expression of what the classical statement means.[7]

The choice is a hard one. If we choose to broaden the metaphorical base of the baptismal formula, we risk the diminishing of the recognition of membership of those we baptize. Such a baptism might not be accepted as valid by some churches. If we choose to retain the traditional formula, we continue the tradition that has valued masculinity higher than femininity. I doubt that this dilemma will soon be solved. Something so crucial as membership and so ancient as the sacrament of baptism will resist change.

I see no choice but to retain classical language in the baptismal formula itself. Full participation in the church's life is at stake, and this factor is of high priority, perhaps even more for women than for men. The rest of the baptismal liturgy, however, makes possible a broadened kind of language. Often, there will be freedom of choice in the scripture readings and hymns. Some of the other prayers provide room for pastoral adaptations. The intractability of the baptismal formula makes it all the more important that imaginative development take place in the other parts of the baptismal liturgy.

While writing this chapter I have realized anew how much the traditional language of Christian worship means to me—and therefore how conservative my instincts are. Phrases and formulas from antiquity have shaped the synapses of my mental life, and thus of my bodily actions too. Only gradually can I repattern the interactions so deeply engrained upon me. Even more deeply engrained are the synapses in the church, a living organism infinitely more complex than the inner life of the single cell of the church which I am.

Changes do take place. Each cell and the organism as a whole are pulled forward by the call of God just as we are fastened to the events long ago in which the same God created us. This tension between memory and hope is always present, always a part of the struggle to be faithful to the past and to the future. In the past, the need to be faithful to our common memory has been the stronger of these two loyalties. It may be that the time will soon be upon us, at least with respect to the language of prayer, when faithfulness to the future will be the more compelling loyalty.

Praise be to you, Infinite God, Architect of this earthly garden which is our home, our working place, our source of continuing pleasure. Because of the overflowing nature of your own inner life, you created this world and all that is in it—

the land and sea and sky,
living creatures of every kind, and plants for beauty and
nourishment,
the seasons with their fluctuations of rest and productivity.
In your own image you created humankind—
male and female so that together we can express the
complexity and creativity of your own self.
And you gave us the care of the world, commanding that we till the
earth, subdue its unruly powers, and use all things as
sacraments of joy, as means of companionship with you.
Praise be to you, Architect of life.

The Dynamics of Change

6

Let the word of Christ dwell in you richly,
teach and admonish one another in all wisdom,
and sing psalms and hymns and spiritual songs
with thankfulness in your hearts to God. (Col. 3:16)

Of the many conversations that have helped shape my convictions concerning liturgical language one stands out with special clarity. In a forum on this topic, a young woman flung out the charge that traditional liturgical language is destructive to human personality and has to be changed immediately. She accused people who resist these changes of being insensitive or of expressing bad faith. When we later talked, I mentioned that it had taken me years to unlearn *thee* and *thou*, and that the change to inclusive language would also take a long time. Crisply stating that she had made the change in a matter of weeks, and that anyone else who wanted to could do the same, she spun around and left the room. Our conversation was over, but the debate continues.

The part of her accusations that stands out most vividly as I remember that incident is the claim that traditional liturgical language is destructive to human personality. Even as a professor of worship, with all of my efforts to affirm the importance of what we say in worship, I had not made so strong a statement about the potency of language used in church. To say that it destroys personality is to claim very much.

Yet it is true that the language of the sanctuary is part of a social system which has systematically given men a place in the world from which women have been barred. Because I was born after the battle over women suffrage, my earliest memories were of both my parents voting (I suspect for Franklin Roosevelt). It came as a shock when I learned along the way that women had enjoyed this degree of citizenship for little more than a decade before my birth. Even though other discriminatory practices have more recently crumbled, the vigorous debates over the Equal Rights Amendment reveal how deeply engrained in our society are the existing patterns of inequality.

Through all this period, the church has been a significant part of the system in which women are kept in perpetually subordinate conditions. Our patterns of life have mirrored those of the society at large. Certain tasks have been designated as belonging to women and others to men. Very little of what we have done has ever questioned the arrangements between the sexes in the larger society.

In fact, the church has helped intensify the problem. Certain texts from the Bible have routinely been exegeted to confirm that God intends men to be dominant and women submissive. The fact that ordinarily only men have been ministers and elders conveys the further conviction that males either are more capable than women or that they in some way express more completely the characteristics of the divine—as though maleness is an essential property of the metaphor that leads us to know God. The supremacy of masculine language makes the point even more completely. All of the above is given divine approval by the things we do and say in services of worship.

The unsatisfactory character of our conventional usage has been made painfully evident to me during several months when I have been following an abridged version of the new *Liturgy of the Hours*. [1] This book provides a pattern of hymns, scripture readings, devotional passages from great Christians, and prayers, all designed to help people in their efforts to praise God. This abridgment bears the subtitle, *Book of Prayer for Personal Use*. The introduction is clear that the liturgy of the hours "is the prayer of the entire people of God" and is "proposed to all the Christian faithful." This translation and abridgment has been prepared by a community of male monks, and the book continuously uses male words instead of inclusive words. All references in readings, instructions, and prayers are to men and brothers rather than to people and friends (or brothers and sisters).

After I had already decided that this fault in the book was so great as to render it unusable in most groups, I came across an even more serious example of entrenched cultural bias. The reading assigned to Monday of Week 11 is Judges 4:1-24. Barak refuses to go into battle unless Deborah the judge goes with him. She agrees to go but tells Barak that as a result he will not gain the glory because Sisera, the leader of the enemy, would fall into the power of a woman. The meditative response provided for this reading is: "God chose the weak of this world to shame the strong, so that mankind can do no boasting before God, for in weakness power reaches perfection."

One of the most poignant expressions of the destruction wrought by traditional cultural patterns is a passage in a badly mildewed book published in 1895, given me by one of my daughters. It was written by the woman for whom her grade school in Indianapolis had been named, Frances E. Willard, and told about her learning to ride a bicycle at the age of 53. In a preliminary comment Willard said that in childhood she had lived a very active life in the country, often imitating her father's work of carpentry and farming. At the age of sixteen "the hampering long skirts were brought, with their accompanying corset and high heels; my hair was clubbed up with pins, and I remember writing in my journal, in the first heartbreak of a young human colt taken from its pleasant pasture, 'Altogether, I recognize that my occupation is gone.'" Willard confessed that she had always been obedient to these limitations, even though she always had "felt their unwisdom even more than their injustice."[2]

The long skirts are gone, except by choice, and jeans rule supreme. Yet the battle of dress codes was fought recently, during the years when my children were in high school. I remember a vivid conversation with a group of parents in a suburban high school on the edge of metropolitan Indianapolis, as recently as 1971, in which they decided that since the mothers wore slacks to the high school basketball games, there was no longer any reason for the dress codes that forced their daughters to wear skirts to the same events. Discrimination continues even though in more subtle ways. It probably will continue that way well into the future since the inertia of humankind is a powerful force. Much disappointment and heartbreak is in store for all of those who commit themselves to the task, as some are doing, of overcoming this inequality in our generation.

Yet my sympathies are on the side of the debate that presses toward equality that is obvious and real. What we do in worship is part of that movement. We can discontinue our destruction of human personality and we can participate in the creation of a new vision of life—God's life and our own—in which reality transcends the fragmentation that is so powerful in current experience. If language can destroy, it can also give life; and that is what I hope will happen as we reform the language of prayer.

By now it is obvious that the process described in this book is slow, a gradual change in prescription rather than a sudden shift in the medication. The interim principle that sums up this aspect of the work can be stated this way: *during this transitional period leaders of worship will work with the natural processes of change.* "Work with" is an ambiguous phrase which includes several phases: understanding the dynamics of human groups, evaluating the adequacy of existing patterns, experimenting with new possibilities, and sharing in the public process of assessing the new developments. This principle has a corollary, a negative form, which is that leaders of worship will try not to frustrate the processes of change. By the word frustrate I mean to include both the effort to keep change from happening and the effort to push change into a rate or pattern that is contrary to its natural rhythms.

How Language Changes

What is spoken inside church buildings is closely related to what is spoken everywhere else. That English does change is clear to anyone who has read a few lines of Chaucer or Shakespeare in high school English literature courses. A comparison of the King James Version of the Bible with any modern translation is almost as dramatic an indication of change. As I compare the slang during my high school days with that of my children during the corresponding years of their lives, I see further evidence of the fact that language changes. The language of prayer also changes, perhaps more slowly, but in ways that parallel the changes in the broader field of language use.

The above paragraph implies that there is one English language. Our ordinary experience teaches us something different, that there are several ways to speak English even in the United States, without adding the further diversity to be found in other parts of the world such as Scotland or Australia. English has variations or dialects, some regional and others identified with social or class groupings. Textbooks do speak of standard English, meaning the dialect spoken by educated and literate people, at least when they are being careful. This standard English has been defined by grammarians, recorded in textbooks, and taught in the schools. In many families, it has been spoken by parents who thus socialized their children to speak that way.

No matter how well people learn standard English, however, they have to struggle to keep it up. One reason for the struggle is the fact that English meaning is conveyed in three ways—by the form of the words (for example, adding an *s* to make the plural of nouns), by the use of function words (such as the helping words that indicate verb tense), and by word order (the arrangement of words in a sentence). Much of classical English grammar, which is used to support standard English, developed in conscious imitation of Latin grammar even though Latin depends primarily upon form to convey meaning, whereas English depends heavily upon word order and function words. Thus, there has always been a struggle to keep grammatical rules and spoken language in harmony. Through the generations the trend in English usage has been away from inflected words, with ever greater dependence upon auxiliary words and word order to convey the meaning of the language.

Often the way we speak standard English differs from the way we use it in more careful and cultivated situations. Yet the conversational form indicates the way the language is moving. For example, in its form *everyone* is singular and grammatical logic requires that the words structurally connected with it also be singular (everyone *wants* to go to Glendale to do *his* shopping). We still feel the singular form of everyone with the verbs, which means that the verb in the example is singular in its form: *everyone wants*; we don't say *everyone want*. The pronoun, however, tends to be plural in form, whatever the grammatical structure of the sentence calls for. Thus many people ordinarily say: *everyone wants to do their shopping*. The plural idea implied in *everyone* wins out and dictates that the plural pronoun be used. Thus the trend with the third-person pronouns seems to be in the direction of what has already happened with second-person pronouns. In common speech and formal speech alike, we now have discontinued several forms of the second-person pronoun, no longer using *thou, ye*, and *thee*, instead using the one word you in all places.

Every generation has its Henry Fowler or Edwin Newman who renews the call to purity of speech. Yet the people continue to talk and write the way they want to, and the language shifts, subtly but surely. Even though I'm a teacher, preacher, and writer, I too have relaxed during the two decades of my professional life, letting current usage influence me so that I am sometimes willing to break the rules that previously I had sought to uphold. No more do I worry so much about sentences missing a vital part, so long as the phrase is carefully crafted; and the agreement of reference pronouns with nouns like none or everyone is something I handle more lightly than I used to.

What seems to be the case is that the people win out over the professors. Journalists and newscasters occupy a middle ground, trying to represent standard English but always in ways that keep them within understanding distance of their publics. Even members of the educational establishment, at least its younger constituents, have relaxed their speech at about the same rate as they have eased up their dress codes.

We feel our way toward new forms, through countless millions of speech transactions, upholding the past and breaking away from it, deliberately trying new ways and accidently falling into them. In time the recorders and arrangers, namely dictionary publishers and grammarians, tell us in their books what we have been doing in our speaking and writings.

This natural process of evolution is being pushed along by the recognition of specific problems in our own time. Whatever the rules have said, the use of the generic masculine has been a limiting factor in experience and understanding; it has contributed to structural bias in culture and in the development of individuals. No longer can we speak the way we have in the past; changes have to be made. Some of the deliberate changes will stick, because they are confirmed by the less conscious processes of linguistic evolution. It is easy enough to change certain titles. Instead of stewardess, flight attendant; instead of manning an enterprise, staffing it; instead of men in the field, representatives or agents. Although man is a convenient word, short, easy to say, easy to rhyme, parallel with words like God and beast, it can easily be replaced with other words or phrases, including humanity, humankind, and the human race.

This more careful selection of words is also a way of dealing with the tendency in speech to belittle women while treating men as fully competent adults. It has been commonplace to use adjectives that call attention to irrelevancies and thus diminish the maturity or competency of the women so described—adjectives that highlight the clothes they are wearing, the way they look, or the surprise that they have conducted themselves so competently. Even worse is the tendency to use belittling nouns: "I'll have my girl do . . . ," when what is meant is secretary. Vocabulary has to be used so as to express the fact that women as well as men belong to the human race, ordinarily are competent adults, and are identified by character and achievement more than by appearance and sex appeal.

I am convinced that most of the changes will take place by bending rules rather than by outright creation of new forms of speech. Perhaps the best illustration is the handling of the problem of third-person singular pronouns to which I referred earlier in my discussion of sermons. The masculine pronoun has consistently been used both when the antecedent noun is known to be a male and when the antecedent noun refers to persons, gender unknown. Only when the antecedent is known to be female, has the pronoun been feminine: "When a nun . . . , she. . . ." Some writers have urged that we invent a new general pronoun that would be used in all such occasions, a pronoun that does not have specific gender references. There does not seem to be any mechanism whereby this kind of invention could take place. In contrast, guidelines now being published move in the direction of staying close to the classical rules while adopting modified patterns. We can regularly say "he or she," or "she or he." Or the pronoun can be made plural—they—on the assumption that what we tend to say in common speech is a sign of the movement of the language toward a single form similar to the emergence of the single form "you" for second-person references.

An even easier way, once we retrain our normal speech patterns, is to cast such sentences in plural forms. In nearly all cases the same meaning is conveyed and the pronoun problem is avoided. In those few instances when the meaning of the sentence requires the use of the singular, the compound pronoun may be used: "he or she."

A more difficult way, especially in conversation or extempore speech, is to recast sentences so that this noun-pronoun construction is not used. In written work, however, where there is time to think and revise, this kind of reconstruction is possible. Gradually, we will come to a place where the unexamined speech forms have moved beyond the older sexist patterns. This movement is very slow, especially for those of us with decades of experience in careful speech. The channels are deeply cut in the processes of the brain. Even when we try to learn a new way of speaking, we are likely to find ourselves starting sentences that are going to be troublesome before they are finished.

How Minds Change

In order for us to adopt a revised way of using standard English, we have to consider how it is that people change in their attitudes and ideas. After all, our goal is for worshipers to use revised texts and procedures willingly and effectively. Furthermore, we hope that the people of the churches will adopt new principles in their efforts to compose prayers and lead worship.

It is clear that all of us are triggered into action by certain kinds of gestures, intonations, phrases, and ideas. Sometimes we have learned to act these ways because of unexamined and unrecognized processes in earlier experience. Hearing the words "let us pray," many Protestants bow their heads and close their eyes without even thinking about their responses, while many Catholics kneel and look toward the altar. We've been taught by word and deed to do what we do. Some of the triggers have been created by specific events in our past experience, events highly charged with emotion. But whatever the origin of the triggers, most of us respond spontaneously in the ways that we have learned.

Some of these mechanisms of response open us to new possibilities and others close us to them. The one kind of response helps us grow even though we may not be ready; the other keeps us from growth even when we need to. A good rate of growth needs to avoid spurts that leave us disjointed. It also needs to avoid artificial and negative restraints that can arise when people close down their receptivity to the continuous transformation of the language of worship.

Since these trigger mechanisms can be so destructive to healthy growth, a good pastoral strategy will try to avoid setting them off. The best way is to introduce additional data without naming it or calling attention to what it is. Often people who are antagonistic to vegetarianism as an ideology are unwilling to sample meatless main dishes. Yet these same people have enjoyed casseroles consisting of vegetables, cereal grains, nuts, cheese, and spices. As their experiences are diversified, they may come to the place where they have more data than their previous explanatory structures can handle. Although they may still oppose the ideology of vegetarianism, they may become able to understand this alternative approach to nourishment and culinary pleasure. They may even be able to discuss the subject in a relaxed and useful way rather than to dismiss it as a foolish point of view.

My strategy with respect to liturgical language is similar. The structure and contents of this book recommend that we enlarge the range of usage and experience without setting off the triggering mechanisms. It tries to present material in ways that are new, nonsexist, and recognizable, but without labeling this material as nonsexist. This approach is one that I believe helps people develop a better vocabulary of prayer without forcing them to brand their former practice as sexist or their later practice as inclusive. As new material comes into use, the people will find that their language stretches for a while, in time stretching so much that they will be able to recognize that something has happened to them. At that point, the processes of interpretation and naming what has happened can be useful. People will be able to use what they know to be inclusive language because they already have been able to try it out before having to worry about its name and emotive character. By avoiding a triggering reaction, they are able to try something for what it is in itself, rather than in its capacity to stimulate a certain kind of reaction.[3]

One difficulty in rewording hymns in the bulletin is that this practice may become a triggering mechanism that distorts growth for many people, causing them to take sides in the debate rather than explore new language because of its usefulness in divine worship.

I have talked about the metaphors that help us know God with several kinds of church groups including Sunday school classes of older adults. It has been interesting to observe the reactions of older women when I tell them that one of the Hebrew words for mercy is rooted in the word for womb. They readily accept my statement that translation usually has lost this female dimension in God's nature. And on some occasions they have taken hold of the idea on their own, suggesting how our understanding of God could be enriched if this aspect of God were more fully expressed in our language of prayer. I suspect, however, that if I had started out the session by labeling current practice as sexist, some of these same people would have been unable to hear my discussion of the womblove of God. Most of these people will probably continue to pray just as they have for the past sixty years and more, calling upon God as Father most of the time. Yet they now are open to the wider character of God and would be able to respond favorably to prayers in which God is spoken to as the One who loves her children just as mothers love the children which they have borne in their wombs.

Language does have to be changed. But the changes should be made in ways that lead to changes in people, too.

How People Change

People do change, awkwardly, in spurts, in their own ways. Sometimes their minds lead the way and the alteration of customs and institutions follows slowly. Frequently, however, the process is reversed and the mental image is the last to change. For a winter I served as the Sunday pastor of a congregation whose Sunday attendance averaged thirty-five persons during that bitter Indiana season. The church was in a small town, off the main highways, and its membership was composed primarily of farmers and factory workers. For reasons that I do not know, and contrary to practice in many other congregations, their organization was inclusive to a high degree. Women and men were included in the eldership and in the office of deacon, which meant that every Sunday at least one woman either offered the eucharistic prayer or in other ways assisted in the administration of the Lord's Supper.[4] The one prominent liturgical function that a woman did not perform, again for reasons I do not know, was as worship leader in the introductory portion of the service. In the spring of that year, they called a woman to be their pastor. The match was a good one, and the congregation has been growing in numbers and in their missional expression of the gospel. Then they realized that their constitution was written in traditional language, which if interpreted strictly would invalidate much of what they had done. This they revised to make it clear that women as well as men were to be elected to the offices of elder and deacon. Furthermore, they inserted inclusive language in the constitution's references to minister so that they could be protected in the future and be free to call either a man or a woman as they chose.

At the same time, people in this congregation have trouble understanding the debate about inclusive language in worship. They resist the ideological movement to design a new way of talking about God and to God. They have told me that they are mystified by my interest in this matter. Clearly, the language of worship will be the last to change, long after other dimensions of their religious reality have altered.

It is not uncommon for small children to form their initial experiences of God in the image of their pastor. Some very unlikely people, as I see them, have reported that little ones in their congregations have called them God. It is known that in the process of abstracting upon experience small children only gradually are able to grasp the structural distinctions between man and woman, uncle and friend, father and mother. These distinctions are too subtle for the very young mind to grasp as it begins to grapple with the patterns of social reality. Thus, the fact that prayer is addressed to Father may be considerably less important than the sex of the person who as minister embodies the divine.

One day I mentioned to my friend now pastoring the Indiana congregation mentioned above that she was going to lead some youngster to confusion. Sooner or later, I told her, some children are going to think of God in womanly form because their minister is a woman. She outpunched me. For nearly a year, she said, one child in her congregation insisted on calling her Jesus, only recently yielding and calling her minister by her own name.

The point of this illustration is stated in a comment which my daughter, Marilyn, wrote into the margin of an earlier draft of this book. "Language naturally changes when it no longer expresses peoples' experiences. Therefore, it *will* change—slowly—to be inclusive when society is inclusive. It will resist change as long as society is in fact not inclusive. Churches which have not already admitted women to full participation need to start there." It seems easy enough for me to agree since in the congregation where I am a member, women serve equally in places of leadership, and in the seminary where I teach a third of the students are women. Yet, I know males dominate faculty and executive staff in my seminary, and in most others. And I hear the arguments against women in ministry, arguments based on divine law as transmitted by the Roman Catholic Church and by Protestant Fundamentalism.[5] I've been in the debate with Bible-believing Christians and know how aggressively they can carry their side of the debate.

God is able to raise up a new generation, as the experiences of the ages demonstrate. What is happening now is that a new generation is arising that hears God calling in new accents. The church is changing, perhaps more swiftly than most people realize; and the new social reality is emerging. The inclusive ecclesial society is going to bring its liturgical confirmation. More and more, the pressure of experience will drive us to a restructuring of how we think and speak.

It is not clear how men and women will be equal, but still unique, in this new social order in the church; nor is it clear how we will resolve the experiments with the language about God and about one another. But the new way of speaking is on its way; and I hope to be here when most folks have learned its accents.

All praise be to you, majestic God, Fountain of life
and Example for us all.
As a shepherd searches for sheep that are lost, so you follow us wherever
*   we go to bring us back to safety.*
As a woman looks into every nook and cranny in order to find the coin
*   which she has lost,*
*   so you look for us in every out-of-the-way place*
*   where we hide from you.*
As a father stands by and waits, longing for his absent son and
*   grieving for his self-righteous one,*
*   so you wait for us while we try our own ways,*
*   only to find that they don't work; so you suffer through our proud*
*   and cruel accusations and help us*
*   discover true humility again.*
Fountain of life and Example for us all, we offer you our praise.

But Are the People Ready?

7

Preach the word, be urgent in season
and out of season, convince, rebuke, and
exhort, be unfailing in patience and in teaching. (II Tim. 4:2)

A high school English teacher phrases the question this way: "Aren't you seminary people pushing an idea that no one else is interested in? Where I teach, people don't pay attention to sexist language. What interests us is access to jobs and equal pay for equal work." A seminary student asks: "Why should I bother with the problem of what to call God? In the church where I work, there's no call for changing liturgical language." The wife of a minister, half-jokingly, asks her husband at a gathering of friends: "Does anyone else in our church agitate for inclusive language? Or am I the only one?"

The unenviable position some pastors occupy was described to me by a United Methodist minister in a midwestern town. At the urging of a few church members, he began to work at the challenge of liturgical language in the way he worded his prayers, in his own speech patterns (especially in sermons), and in his selection of hymns and other worship materials. Everything was working well until several months later a guest preacher commented from the pulpit: "I notice by the prayers and the choice of hymns that your pastor is using inclusive language in your church. I want to express my commendation." That comment was what alerted most members to the fact of inclusiveness in the language in their church, something that most of them had not noticed previously. At first many of them were confused; but then some of them became quite angry.

One conclusion that can be drawn from these examples is that the people aren't ready, that they believe in the existing linguistic patterns, and that they will resist efforts to reform speech in the sanctuary. Again, pastors and musicians face a dilemma. If they use language in the conventional way, they limit its capacity to express the fullness of God's nature, they continue to support a system that treats women and men unfairly, and thus they violate their own consciences and professional obligations. Yet, if they work toward the use of inclusive language, they arouse antagonism among church members and block the ability of many people to worship with their full powers.

This dilemma is similar to one that ministers have confronted in dealing with many other issues—such as Christian responses to the nation's involvement in war, church practices concerning racial integration, and ways of dealing with the energy crisis. It is rare for the people to be *ready* for preaching and programming that lead out toward the reconstruction of attitudes and actions. More common is the readiness to support leadership that seems to support existing patterns, especially when those patterns are threatened by powers that seem very strong.

The underlying question concerns the nature of ministerial leadership. Two types of leadership were contrasted by one columnist who was explaining why a person trained for the ministry could be a good member of the United States Congress but not a good mayor. "As a minister and member of Congress," the columnist stated, "a person's task is to find out what the people want and then help them get it. As mayor, however, a person has to exercise real leadership." I want to disagree with the columnist. Whatever may be the case with members of Congress, ministers also have to exercise what the writer called real leadership.

The major reason for this claim, and at the same time the major element in leadership, is the fact that the proper work of ministers is to find out what God wants and then to help accomplish that divine will. Ministers are officers of the Holy before they are representatives of the people. They are responsible to Christ, the head of the church, more than to the membership of the church. This basic ministerial responsibility expresses itself in several ways. Ministers preach the Word of God. They call the church to responsible Christian practice. They do all within their power to live according to the divine will which they proclaim. They help people respond to the call of God. Part of this ministerial task is to point out sinful behavior; but ministers also help people discover the power to change. It is tempting for us to assume that our ministerial responsibility is fulfilled when we have spoken the truth as we understand it, whether or not the people have heard, understood, and risen to the challenge. Certainly, this degree of faithful performance is important; yet we dare not let go of the goal that human life be transformed and be brought into closer conformity to God's will.

It is undoubtedly true that the people aren't ready for liturgical language that transcends its current fixation upon the metaphors of masculinity. This fact leads to another interim principle: *during this transitional period ministers will have to work with understanding, skill, and persistence in order to assist the completion of the transformation of liturgical language now taking place.* I see several steps in this process.

A Program of Pastoral Action

One step has been described in the earlier chapters of this book, the steady, quiet, adapting of language so that it effectively deals with the needs of our time. All of us control our own use of the English language. In conversation, in announcements, in sermons, we can speak inclusively without asking permission. We can work at it quietly and carefully, gradually feeling our way. Even in churches with prescribed liturgies, we have a considerable range of freedom, including a limited amount of authority to select from the options provided in the official books. And through the years ministers in these churches have exercised freedom to adapt. Even if the salutation in the service book starts out, "My brothers . . ." the priest can say: "My sisters, my brothers. . . ." If they are done gently and naturally, the rightness of such adaptations is readily perceived by the people.

A second step is the development of liturgies that express the evangelical claim that in the economy of God women and men have equal places. An illustration of such a liturgy is one developed by Gail Anderson Ricciuti after realizing that in traditional prayers the models both of righteousness and of sinfulness are almost always men. She decided to construct a responsive prayer of confession and a litany of praise and hope in which a better balance would be expressed. The prayer of confession alternated between brief recitations of sinful actions as described in the Bible—such as Delilah's sin in betraying Samson to his enemies—and unison prayers in which the congregation confesses similar sinfulness— "eager to learn the secrets of others, we misuse our knowledge and bring them to ruin."[1] The litany of praise and hope includes a series of ascriptions, with men beginning "God of the patriarchs . . ." and women continuing "God of the matriarchs. . . ." As the litany progresses, male and female voices continue their alternation, but the sex linkage of their words becomes more complex. The women invoke "God of Abraham, Isaac, and Jacob . . ." and the men call upon "God of Sarah, Rebekah, and Rachel. . . ." The total effect is an amazingly powerful and unifying liturgy of human equality in the presence of the God of our fathers and our mothers.

Another approach is illustrated by Jewish efforts to create contemporary adaptations of traditional liturgies. Although there is a home ceremony celebrating the birth of a son, Jewish tradition has not provided one for the birth of a daughter. One couple set out to remedy that defect by creating a ceremony that is new, "almost revolutional in terms of Jewish tradition."[2]

Vesper services for Advent that I developed in my own church are still another example. On two evenings these candlelight services of praise and prayer were built around the Magnificat. In both cases, the preachers were women in our congregation who were asked to meditate on the experiences of the peasant woman, Mary, and to let their own maternal experiences help them understand her message. Although these services were gentle and compatible with the devotional character of Advent, my intention was to use them as ways of advancing the cause of equality in liturgical practice, both by the fact that women were doing the preaching and by their assignment to use womanly experience as a major source of the message.

A quality which these illustrations share is that all of them are bridge liturgies. They tie together a long-standing tradition, including its ceremonial forms, and new insight and experience. Thus these services are sharply different from those that were especially prominent in the decade of the sixties and which occasionally are repeated even now. The happenings back then cut themselves loose from the tradition, making little effort to connect to familiar patterns of action and beliefs. Instead they sought out novel ideas, methods, forms, and ceremonies. The possibility of bridging two realities was largely discarded. Often confrontation and consciousness-raising were cited as the goals of the services.

The purpose of worship is not to confront or to increase awareness; instead the purpose is to honor God. An agreed-upon pattern of words and actions is used for this purpose. In doing this act, the people themselves are instructed, inspired, and built up in the faith, but these benefits are the corollaries to the major function of the event. Thus, the bridge liturgies function best when they stay within the broad range of the agreements, testing, enlarging, broadening the patterns. The people are the ones who are doing the worshiping, and they will do so only if the words and actions are judged by them to be suitable.

The marriage rite is a liturgy that invites careful pastoral guidance. Its traditional form has expressed a view of subordination—in the woman's pledge to obey and in the entrance rite where she is passed by the father over to the groom, from one guardian to another. The striking of the word *obey* is easily done. Only the most militant biblical literalist is likely to request it; but ministers need not agree, especially if their recommended service does not include that word. The entrance rite is more difficult. Many families will prefer it regardless of what it seems to say about the subordination of women. Ministers will find, when they suggest other ways of coming into the church, that new ways are resisted. Here we are to lead, not drive. With the wedding we can suggest and encourage options. Having done so, we can let the persons most directly involved make the decisions.

A third step in this process is to conduct a careful program of teaching concerning Christian views of the roles of women and men. Our ministerial responsibility for teaching is very high. We help people understand current experience, evaluate it, and make decisions upon it. When issues like the woman's movement arise, it is all the more important that we work at this teaching role. It is amazing how much good is accomplished by balanced explanations of the various positions, of the issues at stake, and of possible resolutions. Ministers need to state their own views, but they can do this gently, firmly, and in a way that permits others to hold contrary views in good faith. We cannot be satisfied with a blunt blurting out of our own views. Rather, our goals need to be serious dialogue, greater understanding, and the possibility of a convergence of minds toward some greater harmony of views.

This mood can carry over into preaching. Again, the "prophet is without honor at home" mentality is too easy an escape into ineffectiveness. It doesn't help much if we merely pour out our ideas and feelings. Preaching still has as a part of its nature the intention to persuade. Some sermonic forms may work better than others when controversial issues are being discussed. A lot of narrative and very little interpretation is one method. What H. Grady Davis calls "a question propounded"[3] is another way that is especially useful when the topic is complicated and controversial. Preachers present the question as clearly and sympathetically as possible; then they work at answering it, proposing and evaluating different ways the issue can be resolved. Sometimes, preachers believe they have an answer that can be recommended; but often they do not yet see their own way, let alone the way for others. Even this kind of preaching, however, can move everyone along through the thicket.

The question of liturgical language is one that needs patient interpretation. People I meet are often frightened or bewildered, and sometimes enraged. Even that rage, however, may be an evidence more of their fear than of their anger. For such people, the emotion is generated by the implication that all they have known of God is being belittled, that the fatherliness of God is being taken away from them, and that some new kind of goddess religion is being shoved off on them by a band of paranoid women. These fears are real, even if not supported by the facts of the debate. In our teaching role, we ministers can help people understand more completely and respond more adequately.

A fourth element in the effort to help people deal with God and one another is to assist them in personalizing prayer. One of my colleagues testified that her meditative reading and praying have been greatly strengthened in this way. In her private religious life, she has a special name for God—one given to her in her own wrestling with the Spirit just as members of a family often have personal names for one another. Regularly she changes "generic masculine" words to "generic feminine," with the result that she now feels included in the Bible as she never had before.

There is no reason that I can see why only women should have the benefit of personalizing private prayer. Men also need to be close enough to God that a special and personal name of the household can emerge. And all of us will benefit by patterns of personal Bible reading that help us receive not only information but also illumination. Jesus set the example. When his disciples asked to be helped with praying, he instructed them, not only with words but also with patterns and disciplines. In every generation ministers serve as guides in prayer, as directors of the religious life, and in this capacity we can offer much help to people who are seeking to transcend the traditional shortcomings of our language.[4]

The fifth aspect of a strong pastoral strategy is to support women in their struggle for equality. In my work as a seminary professor, I read many statements by students describing their pilgrimages of faith. In papers both by men and women certain themes keep coming up, including the search for personal authenticity and Christian identity. Papers written by women frequently are given a particular texture as they describe their childhood experiences of conflict between the call of God which claimed them as Christians and the practical life of the church and society which would not permit them, female as they were, to answer that call completely. These papers describe the new surge of religious power that came when cultural barriers collapsed and they were free to become ministers. Both in their papers and in their activities, some of these women express their desire to help others find this new Christian power; and they speak out vigorously against every hurdle that stands in their way.

I have been deeply moved by these papers and by the testimonies of the living voices of their authors. In similar ways I am touched deeply by women previously unknown to me who have spoken to me in church gatherings, telling of their gratitude for a short essay of mine on inclusive language or for a public comment in some meeting. I admire the courage of these women, my own daughters among them, who are grappling with the principalities and powers of this present darkness (Eph. 6:12) that try to keep them in subjection.

The history of women's movements shows how terrible the odds they face, how grievous the battle, how likely it is that some will be cut down in the struggle. Some of these people have more courage than I and some will be unwise. It is clear to me, however, that the cause is just and that part of our pastoral strategy, whoever we are, must be to uphold them in prayer and in personal relations.

At the same time we are responsible for other people, many of them also women, who cannot join in this movement, who are convinced that the old ways are better. Their consciences and their persons are also to be supported and honored. It is a challenge to every pastor.

Almighty and everliving God, to you we offer praise.
You have revealed yourself as Power . . .
  creating the world and giving life,
  holding all things together despite the forces that
    tear apart and destroy; and
  controlling the march of empires so that the time will come
    when justice prevails over every hateful force.
You have revealed yourself as love . . .
  sending Jesus to show your true nature,
  saving us from our sins, and
  calling us to a new life of servanthood.
You have revealed yourself as Wisdom . . .
  knitting the whole creation together in a wonderful unity,

ministering to us in our estrangement from you and from one
    another, and
reuniting us in your household of faith and good works.
In this house of worship, Infinite Power, Love, and Wisdom . . . we
    all cry "Glory."

How Long the Interim?

8

So let us never tire of doing good, for
if we do not slacken our efforts we shall
in due time reap our harvest. Therefore, as
opportunity offers, let us work for the good of all,
especially members of the household of faith. (Gal. 6:9-10 NEB)

Even with people of good will, good intentions, and good experience, it takes a long time to change patterns of thought and speech. One evening at a church meeting in a working class suburb I saw how slow it is. Around the table sat the elders of the congregation, half a dozen women and men elected to their places of leadership by members of their church. Both members of their pastoral team were there, husband and wife, who preached on alternate Sundays and systematically divided other pastoral duties. All of the vibrations I picked up communicated trust and acceptance. Yet the language of the conversation was largely unreconstructed. In the enthusiasm of the discussion old habits of speech kept coming out again. Preachers were referred to in the singular—and by masculine pronouns. Two or three times during the evening speakers caught themselves and made clumsy but good-natured efforts to make their language match their experience. The time will come when some of these people will learn the new habits. Others will carry to the grave the ways they learned to talk in the earliest years of life.

In this congregation the principle of fairness and faithfulness has been established in policy and in living practice. We now are waiting for speech to catch up . . . and that may take a generation.

The principle has been established in other places too, especially in editorial offices where educational material is prepared. Manuals of style are being changed and manuscripts edited accordingly. We have not worked out all the problems but the directions are clear. Perhaps within a decade much of the change at this level will take place.

Even when printed literature is inclusive, the teachers who use it may not have achieved this same level of adequacy in their habits of thought and speech. Progress will be uneven. In some places teachers and literature will reinforce each other and teaching will become inclusive quickly; in these places the interim will be relatively short. In other places, it will take a longer time to reform practice.

The interim with respect to the liturgy itself will be much longer because of the combination of publishing realities and theological development. All of us depend to some extent upon printed books in our worship endeavors. We use hymnals, directories, manuals, and service books, all of which take time to create, manufacture, distribute, and use up. Half a hundred years—two generations—can easily be required to complete one cycle. The content of these books is studied and evaluated by the church's theologians, by people whose calling and appointment are to expound, interpret, and evaluate the life of faith. We depend on them to help us be faithful to God and to the truth revealed to us.

In North America we are nearing the completion of one cycle of liturgical publication, illustrated by such notable books as *The Book of Common Prayer*, the *Lutheran Book of Worship*, the United Methodist series of *Supplemental Worship Resources*, and the liturgical writings sponsored by the Consultation on Church Union. Although some other processes are under way, the major period of development has reached a time of quiet.

Meantime other developments are occurring. A revised and inclusive translation of the Bible, or at least of the readings of the lectionary, is getting started. One or two churches are now beginning work on new worship books which can help us advance another step. Individuals are developing provisional services and orders that explore new possibilities for the form of services and language of prayers.

The interim period will include a long and sustained theological endeavor. This theological work may take longer than any of the other aspects of this new challenge because the questions which we must now reconsider penetrate to the very center of our faith, dealing with the nature of God, with good and evil, with human nature, and with ecclesiology. Indeed, it may be that the stimulus to theological reflection may be the most important outcome of the current discussion of the language of prayer.

By its very nature the scholarly process moves carefully, step by step, gathering in the data, and gradually creating new harmonies. Judging by conversations with colleagues on my own campus and by movements of thought in other groups with which I meet, this process is under way. I hope for significant results in time to come.

Another aspect of this interim is also hard to anticipate. I do not know how long it will take for women to become as prominent as men in the liturgical life of congregations. The movement will be more in lurches than measured steps. Some of the congregations in my own church which now elect women to the eldership are finding that they have to develop informal guidelines to keep a reasonable number of men in that high congregational office. I suspect that a similar phenomenon will begin to develop at entry-level pastoral positions in some denominations. We may have a substantial body of women in church leadership much sooner than some people expect.

These factors lead me to the conclusion that the interim will be poorly defined. We will make our ways through it at differing rates of speed and emerge on the other side perhaps without realizing it.

Now is not the time to be concerned with the length of the interim. Now is the time to enter into the work of liturgical reform. There is work to do; and the interim will close when our work has been completed. "Therefore . . . be steadfast, immovable, always abounding in the work of the Lord, knowing that in the Lord your labor is not in vain" (I Cor. 15:58).

Gracious God, Friend to those who turn to you,
    may your Name be praised.
You do not remember the sins we committed when we were
        young—
the rebellions, the angers, the fears, the impetuous actions of the
    immature.

Instead, you think of us in the light of your own goodness and love,
always seeing the promise rather than the partial performances,
always holding before us possibilities rather than the
achievements with which we are satisfied.

Even when we choose to disobey, your friendship remains unswerving:
in your love and faithfulness you forgive us;
you renew your covenant and reaffirm the testimonies to your
commandments.

When we are alone, or when enemies rise up against us,
you do not abandon us. You come to our rescue with encouragement.
Your integrity and uprightness inspire us with new hope and new
courage.
We trust in you and are protected in our time of trouble.

Divine Friend, may your Name be praised.

Workbook for the
Lord's Day Service:
Examples and Explanations

9

The test of theory is practice. What we do in real life demonstrates the extent to which our general principles interpret experience and help us develop it further. The purpose of this "workbook" is to show my own efforts to develop liturgical materials according to principles discussed in this book. I have chosen to present preliminary possibilities, with comments and explanations, rather than finished examples, in the hope that they will help readers think through the process of converting principles into practice.

Our challenge is to start with a fixed body of liturgical material and develop a pattern of words and actions that moves beyond certain linguistic and theological characteristics of that inheritance. While making this move we must retain authenticity—by being faithful to our inheritance and fair to the pastoral realities which we as ministers and musicians face.

The major part of this workbook presents adaptations of the psalms appointed for Sunday worship. These Hebrew lyrics have been a staple in Christian worship throughout much of the church's life. Although they are less often used in the churches that favor extempore prayer, there is a serious effort even in these church bodies to recover the Psalter. This effort is to be encouraged at a time when so many worship leaders have been casting about for responsive readings. The Sunday bulletins I see often use newly composed material, most of which (even that which comes from published sources) is insipid, hortatory, clever, or in some other way too thin for an act as important as Christian public worship.

These selections from the Psalter have been adapted and arranged for congregational use. My intention is that they can become the instrument for the people's worship at several points in the liturgy.

The Introduction. These selections can be used as responsive sentences of worship at the beginning of the service. They establish the tone for the day's liturgy, actively engage leaders and congregation, and express the kerygmatic nature of worship. They focus attention on God but in such a way that the subjective interest of the worshipers is also made evident.

Service of the Word. It has long been customary for psalms to be recited as counterpoint to the reading of the scripture lessons. In this way biblical narrative and teaching are permeated by praise so that the entire service of the Word becomes a testimony to our adoration of the God whose self-revelation is summarized in the Bible. Often the psalm has come between the Old Testament and Epistle readings; but other patterns could also be followed.

The Prayers of the People. The classical shape of Christian worship, begun in the synagogue and continued in the church, moves from an introduction of praise, through the service of the Word, to the congregation's words and actions of yielding themselves back to God. Indeed, this response of self-offering, this sacrifice of praise and thanksgiving, can be looked upon as the final and climactic act of the liturgy. Yet, it also is the one which usually is least adequate in its character and form. The typical Protestant service gives such a poor instrument for congregational response to the Word of God that a vast number of people are consistently denied this aspect of Christian worship.

One use that could be made of these psalm arrangements is to make them a major part of the post-sermon congregational liturgy of praise and petition. They will be followed by other prayers. The offering of money, and other ceremonies, could also be included in this part of the service.

Ministers and musicians always work within a framework that shapes their creativity. Even in the churches of the extempore traditions in America, certain structures exist that control the choices. In my work, this fact is also true. The ones within which I work, and which have helped shape the following examples, can be summarized with three guidelines.

First, the traditional calendar of the church is the major element for organizing time. Advent, Christmas, Epiphany, Lent, Easter, and Pentecost are the divisions of the year. Each one expresses the full mystery of our salvation; yet each one also accents a particular part of the whole.

Second, the ecumenical lectionary provides the pattern of Bible reading and sermon material for my Sunday liturgical activity. I frequently serve as Sunday *ad interim* pastor for Disciple congregations in Central Indiana and my consistent practice has been to develop new sermons on lectionary texts just as I would if I were to be pastor on a more permanent basis. These interim periods range in length from three months to a year, which means that I have the opportunity to test the lectionary approach fairly extensively. During my most recent period of such service, which lasted for eight months, I followed the version of the lectionary published in *The Book of Common Prayer* (1977). This book has adopted a pattern for Pentecost that is synchronized with the Roman Catholic schedule. In contrast to some other variants of this lectionary, the one in *The Book of Common Prayer* appoints one psalm for each Sunday and it is used in all three cycles of the lectionary.

Third, the pattern of liturgical material should be adaptable to varied circumstances. Some congregations are well endowed musically and can sing the psalms even when translated in unmetrical lines. Or there may be soloists or choir able to sing certain lines while the congregation says others. These examples are set forth so that they can be used in several ways, either sung or said: (a) leader and congregation can recite the thematic verses at the beginning, between divisions, and at the end of the psalm; and they can sing the psalm itself; (b) leader and congregation can recite the thematic verses while singers sing the psalm; (c) leader and congregation can recite both the responsive verses and the psalm. It is my assumption that there are circumstances that would lead some worship leaders to use only one of the psalm divisions provided.

Christian liturgical practice has long followed the custom of using thematic verses (often called antiphons) as a way of highlighting one of the motifs in a psalm or reading. Usually drawn from Scripture, thematic verses provide a biblical commentary on itself. By changing thematic verses, we are able to suit a psalm to the various moods and movements of the liturgy of time. I have developed the thematic verses from the Bible readings assigned for each of the Sundays of that season (except where the exhibit indicates otherwise).

My choice of psalms was determined primarily by the readiness with which they can be adapted by the interim principles discussed in this book. I have preferred second-person psalms; and I have tended to omit many of the difficult verses. My intention has been to select material that is authentic to the ancient tradition, adapted to the seasons of the year and arranged so that it is faithful to God and fair to the people.

The psalm prayers have been composed according to the following method. I have selected an attribute of God that is featured in the psalm, using that as the source of the divine epithet. The text of the prayer recites God's actions, referring to the way that Jesus fulfills them, and asks that God continue to work in us today. It is my hope that these prayers will serve as the invocation (which for most Protestants is defined as the short prayer at the beginning of the service), as the prayer for illumination prior to reading the Bible, or as a prayer said during the major period of prayer following the sermon.

I am working with the version of the Psalter developed for *The Book of Common Prayer* (1977). It is contemporary in its diction, designed for liturgical use, and sensitive to the need for inclusive language. The exhibits select portions of these prayer book psalms, printing them without adaptation, except for abridgment. In the notes following each season, I comment on ways of dealing with some of the problems that remain.

As they now stand, these examples retain a few masculinities, a few instances where God is referred to with a third-person pronoun or generic language is used for persons. Even if these examples are used as they now stand, the result would be a language of prayer that moves far down the road toward the goal of being inclusive. If adapted according to my notes, the advance is even farther.

One title for God that frequently appears is Lord. In nearly every case the Hebrew uses the name of God YHWH, which current scholars spell out as Yahweh. We have to make a choice. Either we pronounce the name that Jews have always been unwilling to pronounce. Or we use an agreed-upon euphemism. The Hebrew choice was to say Lord—and that is the course of action adopted here. My justification is that in American use of the language, Lord no longer is gender-specific as it once was. Could other euphemisms be chosen? I suppose so. The one that for Christians would be most easily established, indeed already is in place, is Father. Yet, this term creates even more serious difficulties than Lord. Although I admit the problematic character of Lord, I have chosen to retain it in these psalms.

How free are we to make liturgical adaptations of biblical language? Through the years, the church has been quite strict in its reading of the lections. In its acclamations, prayers, and hymns, however, there has been a fairly substantial readiness to adapt biblical language without being bound to strict textual accuracy. The thematic verses are close to scripture, but frequently altered. I have been less ready to do the same with psalm texts. My notes suggest a few possibilities, some of which I am willing to do in my own practice. I would try in the citation always to indicate that the text is *adapted* from the psalm cited.

Although I have done extensive testing of another body of liturgical material illustrative of the principles in this book, the examples in this exhibit are not tested. I don't know how well they would serve a congregation. I provide them not so much because they show the best route but because they provide another way for ministers and musicians to think through the ways to transform their current liturgical practice.

Advent

Psalm 146:1-9

Comments on the Psalm and Its Arrangement[1]

This psalm is an eloquent testimony to God who is the gracious Helper of the weak. For that reason it is a fitting element for the season of Advent when the church yearns for its release from the bondage of sin and the terror of history. The text makes clear that religion and life are intertwined, that salvation is both inner and outer. Therefore, this psalm makes a strong contribution to Advent liturgies which in many churches are naïve celebrations of life's pleasantries.

I have included the full text of the psalm even though the Prayer Book translation retains two third-person pronouns for God (divisions B and C). The superiority of this translation over the Revised Standard Version is shown by its use of rulers instead of princes, child of earth instead of son of man (division A), and the use of plural forms instead of singular (happy are they, division B). The Revised Standard Version, however, reads "who keeps faith for ever," thus avoiding one of the pronouns for God. I would be inclined to use the RSV's rendering for that line and substitute the Lord for he in division C.

The Psalm Arrangement

L They shall beat their swords into plowshares,
   and their spears into pruning hooks;
R nation shall not lift up sword against nation,
   neither shall they learn war any more. (Isa. 2:4)

   A. Hallelujah!
       Praise the Lord, O my soul!*

I will praise the Lord as long as I live;
I will sing praises to my God while I have my being.
Put not your trust in rulers, nor in any child of earth,*
for there is no help in them.
When they breathe their last, they return to earth,*
and in that day their thoughts perish.

(Thematic Verse)

B.   Happy are they who have the God of Jacob for their help!*
whose hope is in the Lord their God;
Who made heaven and earth, the seas, and all that is in them;*
who keeps his promise for ever;
Who gives justice to those who are oppressed,*
and food to those who hunger.

(Thematic Verse)

C.   The Lord sets the prisoners free;
the Lord opens the eyes of the blind;*
the Lord lifts up those who are bowed down;
The Lord loves the righteous;
the Lord cares for the stranger;*
he sustains the orphan and widow,
but frustrates the way of the wicked.
The Lord shall reign for ever,*
your God, O Zion, throughout all generations.
Hallelujah!

L They shall beat their swords into plowshares,
and their spears into pruning hooks;
R nation shall not lift up sword against nation,
neither shall they learn war any more. (Isa. 2:4)

Faithful God, Helper of the children of earth, we offer you our
praise. By the word of prophets you promised to rescue us
from the terrors of this world; and by the life of Jesus
you keep your word. Help us to believe your promises and
to find our life in you.
Helper of the children of earth, we offer you our praise.

Thematic Verses for the Sundays of Advent (Cycle A)

First Sunday of Advent (selected from Isa. 2:4)
    L   They shall beat their swords into plowshares,
        and their spears into pruning hooks;
    R   nation shall not lift up sword against nation,
        neither shall they learn war any more.

Second Sunday of Advent (selected from Isa. 11:9)
    L   The earth shall be full of the knowledge of the Lord
    R   as the waters cover the sea.

Third Sunday of Advent (selected from Isa. 35:4)
    L   Be strong, fear not!
    R   Behold, your God will come and save you.

Fourth Sunday of Advent (selected from Isa. 7:14)
    L   It is God who gives the sign;
        A young woman shall conceive and bear a son;
    R   And his name shall be called Immanuel.

Christmas

Psalm 98:5-10

Comments on the Psalm and Its Arrangement

This psalm is one of those enthronement psalms which *The Book of Common Prayer* appoints for the Christmas season. All of them seem to derive from an annual service celebrating Yahweh's enthronement as sovereign over Israel. They are difficult to use because of their structure—all cast in third-person singular. If the psalms are understood as applying to Jesus, that form is manageable, but if to Yahweh, we face the problem of masculine language. These psalms are suitable for Christmas, because they affirm so triumphantly that God is acting for our salvation.

The excerpts chosen in this exhibit use the portions of the psalm that are most consistent with the interim principles I am recommending. They are addressed primarily to the congregation, urging a joyful offering of praise to God who is our sovereign ruler.

The first portion of the psalm, which I have omitted, features the metaphor of God as victor in warfare, an image that I find difficult to use.

Division A calls God king, a title that is consistent with the occasion when this psalm was used long ago. That verse could be omitted. Some might choose to use a parallel term such as monarch, ruler, or sovereign.

The Jerusalem Bible has only one pronoun in division B: "at the presence of Yahweh, for he comes to judge the earth, to judge the world with righteousness and the nations with strict justice." The first line of that stanza could be altered to read: "at the presence of the Lord, who comes."

The Psalm Arrangement

L   The people who walked in darkness have seen a great light;
R   Those who dwelt in a land of deep darkness, on them has light shined (Isa. 9:2).

A.   Shout with joy to the Lord, all you lands;*
         lift up your voice, rejoice, and sing.
      Sing to the Lord with the harp,*
         with the harp and the voice of song.
      With trumpets and the sound of the horn*
         shout with joy before the King, the Lord.
(Thematic Verse)
B.   Let the sea make a noise and all that is in it,*
      the lands and those who dwell therein.

Let the rivers clap their hands,*
    and let the hills ring out with joy before the Lord,
    when he comes to judge the earth.
In righteousness shall he judge the world*
    and the peoples with equity.

L The people who walked in darkness have seen a great light;
R Those who dwelt in a land of deep darkness, on them has light
    shined (Isa. 9:2).

Joyful God, Composer of the music of the spheres, we sing and play
    our adoration. When you created the universe, the morning
      stars sang out together; and when you sent Jesus to be
        born of Mary, the angelic chorus sang out your message
          of peace and good will. By your word, teach us your
            commandments and by your indwelling Spirit inspire
          us to perform your songs of Zion.
Composer of the music of the spheres, to you we shout with joy.

Thematic Verses for the Season of Christmas (Cycle A)

Christmas Day (selected from Isa. 9:2)
    L The people who walked in darkness have seen a great light;
    R those who dwelt in a land of deep darkness, on them has
       light shined.

First Sunday after Christmas (selected from Isa. 61:11)
    L As the earth brings forth its shoots,
    R so God will cause righteousness and praise to spring forth
       before all the nations.

Second Sunday after Christmas (selected from Jer. 31:13-14)
    L I will turn your mourning into joy, says the Lord.
    R I will comfort you and give you gladness for sorrow.

Epiphany

Psalm 89:1-2, 8, 14, 15-17

Comments on the Psalm and Its Arrangement

The excerpts in this exhibit are chosen from the first part (vv. 1-18) of this long psalm, which contains a hymn in praise of God. It may have been used in services that featured the renewing of the covenant with God. The suitability of this psalm for Epiphany, the season of Christ's manifestation to the world, is subtle, suggested especially in the second couplet of division A.

Often thematic verses are selected from the psalm itself rather than from other scriptural sources, and I have followed that pattern here. Even in years when Easter comes early, there will be more than two Sundays. Thus, additional thematic verses will need to be selected, either from the psalm or from the readings assigned to the Sundays of this season.

In division B God is compared to other heavenly beings and found to be superior. Some interpreters are troubled by this kind of competitive evaluation, seeing in it evidence that masculine traits of God are more than problems of the language but are problems in our basic understanding of God's own nature. People who hold this point of view may choose to omit that verse.

Note the personifications of the divine character in division B—righteousness, justice, love, and truth.

The Psalm Arrangement

L   The heavens bear witness to your wonders, O Lord,
R   and to your faithfulness in the assembly of the holy ones,

   A.   Your love, O Lord, for ever will I sing;*
        from age to age my mouth will proclaim your
        faithfulness.

For I am persuaded that your love is established for ever;*
you have set your faithfulness firmly in the heavens.
(Thematic Verse)
B.   Who is like you, Lord God of hosts?*
O mighty Lord, your faithfulness is all around you.
Righteousness and justice are the foundations of your
throne;*
love and truth go before your face.
(Thematic Verse)
C.   Happy are the people who know the festal shout!*
they walk, O Lord, in the light of your presence.
They rejoice daily in your Name;*
they are jubilant in your righteousness.
For you are the glory of their strength,*
and by your favor our might is exalted.

L   The heavens bear witness to your wonders, O Lord,
R   and to your faithfulness in the assembly of the holy ones.

Holy God, Ruler of heaven and earth, we proclaim your
faithfulness.
In all of the generations of time your righteousness and justice,
your love, and truth, have been shown superior to the
heavenly creatures and to the powers of the created world.
And in Jesus' own life you have revealed
these aspects of your character to us.
By your word in Scripture, teach us obedience and trust
so that we will be more like you.
Ruler of heaven and earth, we proclaim your faithfulness.

Thematic Verses for Epiphany (Cycle A)

Number 1 (selected from Ps. 89:5)
L   The heavens bear witness to your wonders, O Lord,
R   And to your faithfulness in the assembly of the holy ones.

Number 2 (selected from Ps. 89:11)
    L   Yours are the heavens; the earth also is yours;
    R   You laid the foundations of the world and all that is in it.

Lent

Psalm 19:7-14

Comments on the Psalm and Its Arrangement[1]

This psalm contains two hymns united into one act of praise. Verses
1-6 are in praise of nature and verses 7-14 are in praise of the law of
God. I have selected the second of these hymns because it suggests one
of the themes of Judaism that all too often has been suppressed in
Christianity. As Artur Weiser puts the matter: "In the law the will of
God is manifested to educate and to save, and for that reason it is also
the basis of a firm trust in the lovingkindness of God. Every sentence of
the psalm resounds with this note of joyous confidence."[2] Christianity
is an ethical religion, and the season when we are especially conscious
both of Jesus' example of obedience and our own baptismal vows is a
good time to rehearse this fact.

The one awkward section is in the first line of division C: "Who
can tell how often he offends?" Clearly this section is individualized,
which makes it difficult to shift to a plural form. Yet this kind of
generic masculine is clearly inadequate according to the canons now
developing. In ordinary prose, I would simply add the feminine:
". . . he or she. . . ." Here, I hesitate. The problem is not in adding
to the text since even the masculine pronoun is supplied by
translation. Rather, it is that the phrase seems so uncharacteristic of
biblical style. So far, I have not seen another way of casting the lines
that retain the purpose and their power.

The Psalm Arrangement

L Let the words of my mouth and the meditation of my heart
be acceptable in your sight,
R O Lord, my strength and my redeemer,

   A. The law of the Lord is perfect
       and revives the soul;*
   the testimony of the Lord is sure
       and gives wisdom to the innocent.
The statutes of the Lord are just
       and rejoice the heart;*
   the commandment of the Lord is clear
       and gives light to the eyes.
The fear of the Lord is clean
       and endures forever;*
   the judgments of the Lord are true
       and righteous altogether.

(Thematic Verse)

   B. More to be desired are they than gold,
       more than much fine gold,*
   sweeter far than honey,
       than honey in the comb.
By them also is your servant enlightened,*
   and in keeping them there is great reward.

(Thematic Verse)

   C. Who can tell how often he offends?*
   cleanse me from my secret faults.
Above all, keep your servant from presumptuous sins;
let them not have dominion over me;*
   then shall I be whole and sound,
   and innocent of a great offense.

L Let the words of my mouth and the meditation of my heart be
acceptable in your sight,
R O Lord, my strength and my redeemer.

Almighty God, our Strength and our Redeemer, we honor you. You
have given us the law of life to guide and uphold us through
all our days. By the word of prophets and apostles, you
teach us its beauty and its power. And in Jesus Christ
you show us your true nature as source of everything
that is strong and desirable.
O Lord, Strength and Redeemer, we honor you.

Thematic Verses for Lent (Cycle A)

General (selected from Ps. 19:14)
    L Let the words of my mouth and the meditation of my heart
        be acceptable in your sight,
    R O Lord, my strength and my redeemer.

First Sunday in Lent (selected from Rom. 5:11)
    L We rejoice in God through our Lord Jesus Christ,
    R through whom we have now received our reconciliation.

Second Sunday in Lent (selected from John 3:17)
    L For God sent the Son into the world, not to condemn the
        world,
    R but that the world might be saved through him.

Third Sunday in Lent (selected from Rom. 5:1)
    L Since we are justified by faith,
    R we have peace with God through our Lord Jesus Christ.

Fourth Sunday in Lent (selected from Eph. 5:1-2)
    L Be imitators of God, as beloved children.
    R And walk in love, as Christ loved us and gave himself up for
        us, a fragrant offering and sacrifice to God.

Fifth Sunday in Lent (selected from Rom. 6:23)
    L The wages of sin is death,
    R but the free gift of God is eternal life in Christ Jesus our
        Lord.

Sixth Sunday in Lent (selected from Isa. 45:22)
   L   Turn to me and be saved, all the ends of the earth!
   R   For I am God, and there is no other.

Easter

Psalm 118:5-9, 16-17, 22-24

Comments on the Psalm and Its Arrangement

This psalm is a strong illustration of the task of transcending the metaphors of masculinity. It is a vigorous poetical declaration of praise; and its liturgical character is evident. Through the generations it has been understood as especially applicable to Christ. Yet, this psalm depends heavily upon masculinities, both in grammatical form and in some of its figures of speech. The process of selection has to be exercised carefully. I have sidestepped the problem by omitting the litany (vv. 1-4), and by choosing portions that highlight the Easter notes of God's triumph over death.

The Psalm Arrangement

L   You are my God, and I will thank you;
R   You are my God, and I will exalt you.
     Hosanna!

   A.   I called to the Lord in my distress;*
           the Lord answered by setting me free.
        The Lord is at my side, therefore I will not fear;*
           what can anyone do to me?
        The Lord is at my side to help me;*
           I will triumph over those who hate me.

(Thematic Verse)
B. It is better to rely on the Lord*
    than to put any trust in flesh.
    It is better to rely on the Lord*
    than to put any trust in rulers.

(Thematic Verse)
C. The right hand of the Lord has triumphed!*
    the right hand of the Lord is exalted!
    the right hand of the Lord has triumphed!
    I shall not die, but live,*
    and declare the works of the Lord.

(Thematic Verse)
D. The same stone which the builders rejected*
    has become the chief cornerstone.
    This is the Lord's doing,*
    and it is marvelous in our eyes.
    On this day the Lord has acted;*
    we will rejoice and be glad in it.

L   You are my God, and I will thank you;
R   you are my God, and I will exalt you.
    Hosanna!

Merciful God, our Strength and our Song, we give thanks to you.
    When you raised Jesus from the dead you triumphed over all
    the powers of evil that hem us in on every side. You are
    our salvation. On this glorious day, shine upon us with
    the light of life and fill us with wisdom and strength.
Our Strength and our Song, we give thanks to you.

Thematic Verses for the Season of Easter (Cycle A)

General (selected from Ps. 118:28)
L   You are my God, and I will thank you;
    you are my God, and I will exalt you.
    Hosanna!

Easter Day (selected from Col. 3:2-3)
> L Set your minds on things that are above, not on things that are on earth.
> R For you have died, and your life is hid with Christ in God. Hosanna!

Second Sunday of Easter (selected from Ps. 16:11)
> L You will show me the path of life;
> R in your presence there is fullness of joy. Hosanna!

Third Sunday of Easter (selected from I Peter 1:21)
> L Through Jesus we have confidence in God,
>   who raised him from the dead and gave him glory,
> R so that our faith and hope are in God.

Fourth Sunday of Easter (selected from I Peter 2:24)
> L He himself bore our sins in his body on the tree,
>   that we might die to sin and live to righteousness.
> R By his wounds we have been healed.

Fifth Sunday of Easter (selected from I Peter 2:2)
> L Like newborn babes, we long for the pure spiritual milk
>   that by it we may grow up to salvation.
> R For we have tasted the kindness of the Lord. Hosanna!

Sixth Sunday of Easter (selected from I Peter 3:18)
> L Christ died for our sins, once for all,
>   the righteous for the unrighteous,
> R That he might bring us to God. Hosanna!

Seventh Sunday of Easter (selected from John 17:3)
> L And this is eternal life, that we know you the only true God,
> R And Jesus Christ whom you have sent, Hosanna!

NOTES

Chapter 1 The Challenge to Conventional Language

1. The literature in the field of women and religion is growing rapidly and cannot be listed here. A sample of relevant titles is published in *Language About God in Liturgy and Scripture: A Study Guide*, edited by Barbara A. Withers (Philadelphia: The Geneva Press, 1980). I have found four volumes to be especially useful because they contain collections of essays representing a wide body of opinion. *Sexist Religion and Women in the Church*, edited by Alice L. Hageman in collaboration with the Women's Caucus of Harvard Divinity School (New York: Association Press, 1974) contains essays by ten writers. An international perspective is provided by the October 1975 issue (Vol. XXVII, No. 4) of *The Ecumenical Review* which contains eight essays by scholars from around the world and a working paper of the World Council of Churches on "The Community of Women and Men in the Church." A more diverse and aggressive, and therefore more useful, collection of essays is contained in *Womanspirit Rising: A Feminist Reader in Religion*, edited by Carol P. Christ and Judith Plaskow (New York: Harper & Row, 1979). Included in this volume are several of the groundbreaking essays in the recent women's movement. Another volume that is useful in this more general way is *Sistercelebrations: Nine Worship Services*, edited by Arlene Swidler (Philadelphia: Fortress Press, 1974). Although the main contents of the book are the services, the introductory essays are illuminating. The book which for many people opened the door to the topic of worship that transcends its masculine bondage is *Women and Worship: A Guide to Non-Sexist Hymns, Prayers, and Liturgies*, by Sharon Neufer Emswiler and Thomas Neufer Emswiler (New York: Harper & Row, 1974). Their more recent book is *Wholeness in Worship* (New York: Harper & Row, 1980). One of the most practical discussions of ways to improve practical religious language is Marianne Sawicki's *Faith and Sexism: Guidelines for Religious Educators* (New York: The Seabury Press, 1979).

2. The notable examples of new worship books are *The Book of Common Prayer*, According to the Use of The Episcopal Church (New York: The Church Hymnal Corporation and The Seabury Press, 1977); the *Lutheran Book of Worship* (Minneapolis: Augsburg Publishing House; and Philadelphia: Board of Publication, Lutheran Church in America, 1978); Supplemental Worship Resources, a series of books developed by The United Methodist Church (Nashville: Abingdon, various dates); and the liturgical publications of the Roman Catholic Church.

3. I am prompted to use the words reformist and revolutionary by the introductory essay in *Womanspirit Rising* (see note 1), pp. 9-10.

Chapter 2 Faithful and Fair

1. An example is an article by Joseph W. Schneider and Sally L. Hacker, "Sex Role Imagery and Use of the Generic 'Man' in Introductory Texts: A Case in the Sociology of Sociology," *The American Sociologist* 8 (1973), 12-18. The authors conclude: "Our research challenges use of the generic term, 'man,' in introductory sociology texts. We argue that this term, contrary to its formal definition, is not in fact interpreted to mean 'people' or 'human beings,' but rather cues students to think 'male,' p. 12. We argue that 'man' may be seen as a symbol of male dominance both in the larger society and in the discipline of sociology, and that its continued use could serve to perpetuate and reinforce that condition."

2. I have taken this information from *Companion to Hymnbook for Christian Worship*, edited by Arthur N. Wake (St. Louis: Bethany Press, 1970), pp. 290-91.

3. Romans 16:1 mentions Phoebe who is called *diakonon*. Here as elsewhere in the New Testament, this word is masculine. Even so, it has often been translated deaconess. Translators and editors of dictionaries seem to be perplexed by the fact that a woman is called by a term which in later church history was used exclusively for males.

4. For the interpretation of the missionary movement, I have depended upon "Women and Missions: The Cost of Liberation," in *Sexist Religion and Women in the Church* (see note 1, chapter 1), pp. 167-93.

5. One of the most useful books is *Words and Women*, by Casey Miller and Kate Swift (Garden City, N.Y.: Doubleday & Co., 1976). It discusses and illustrates problems with traditional usage, suggests corrective measures, and includes bibliographical notes.

6. For convenient discussions of the name of God, see: John L. McKenzie, S.J., "Some Aspects of Old Testament Thought," *The Jerome Biblical Commentary*, edited by R. S. Brown, S.S., *et. al.* (Englewood Cliffs, N.J.: Prentice-Hall, 1968), II, 736-67; James Muilenburg, "The History of the Religion of Israel," *The Interpreter's Bible* (Nashville/New York: Abingdon-Cokesbury Press, 1952) I, pp. 292-348; B. W. Anderson, "God, Names Of," *The Interpreter's Dictionary of the Bible* (Nashville: Abingdon, 1962) II, pp. 407-17; and "God, O.T. View Of," pp. 417-30.

7. Anderson, *The Interpreter's Dictionary of the Bible*, II, p. 413.

8. Helmer Ringgren, *Word and Wisdom: Studies in the Hypostatization of Divine Qualities and Functions in the Ancient Near East* (Lund: Hakan Ohlssons Boktryckeri, 1947). This highly technical study explores the origin of polytheism: which came first, one god or many gods? Ringgren points to the priority of the one god, showing how the many gods are the result of a process whereby the attributes of that one god are given form and independent life.

9. Two constructive statements that are illustrative of new possibilities are *God As Spirit*, by G. W. H. Lampe (New York: Oxford University Press, 1978), and *The Feminine Dimension of the Divine*, by Joan Chamberlain Engelsman (Philadelphia: The Westminster Press, 1979). Lampe is a noted patristic scholar whose interest is quite different from the feminist questions with which I am dealing. Even so, his reopening of the trinitarian discussions can be a very helpful contribution to the new theological discussion. Engelsman uses Jungian archetypes as the paradigm for reviewing biblical teachings about God and proposing next steps.

In his chapter on "Spirit" in *Doxology: The Praise of God in Worship, Doctrine and Life* (New York: Oxford University Press, 1980) Geoffrey Wainwright mentions that worship is "once more inviting the theologians to rethink the doctrine of God" (p. 96). He calls attention to the fact that the place of the Holy Spirit in the Trinity came about more as the result of "theological reflexion" than of "popular devotion." "Would things have gone differently," he asks, "if the feminizing of the Holy Spirit found in Syrian gnosticism had made its way more widely?" (p. 103).

Chapter 3 Sovereignty and Intimacy

1. The "interplay" between worship and doctrine is subtle and complex. Although more often treated by Catholic writers, a few Protestant writers also have discussed the influence that worship should have over doctrine and the control that doctrine should have over worship. A very careful discussion of historical and systematic aspects of this interplay is found in Geoffrey Wainwright's *Doxology: The Praise of God in Worship, Doctrine and Life* (New York: Oxford University Press, 1980), pp. 218-83. I am recommending a more experimental course of action than Wainwright considers appropriate. He says, "At this time . . . it is important that official liturgical revision should err on the conservative side, if the faith is to be transmitted through a period of reductionism into a time when an adequate reformulation of its substance may take place. It is never the function of *avant-garde* theologians to control the public worship of the Church" (p. 344). Wainwright introduces as an example of the dangers John Killinger's *Leave It to the Spirit* which I also shy away from. I too was increasingly hostile to the celebrationist movement of the 1960s. That movement, it seemed to me, lacked maturity both in doctrine and in worship, neither partner strong enough to influence the other. The doctrinal relaxation I am calling for at this time is limited in scope. It is the recommendation that we be less vigorous in applying formal requirements—rubrics perhaps is the appropriate term—so that piety nourished by Scripture and Christian experience, as well as by current theological endeavor, can develop more fully. Of course, systematic theological endeavor must continue at the same time. The interplay of doctrine and worship must continue.

2. One example of this elevated language is the prologue to the divine liturgy. "It is meet and right that we should laud thee, bless thee, praise thee, give thanks unto thee, and adore thee in all places of thy dominion: for thou art God ineffable, incomprehensible, invisible, inconceivable; thou art from everlasting and art changeless, thou, and thine Only-begotten Son, and thy Holy Spirit . . ." *Service Book of the Holy Orthodox—Catholic Apostolic Church*, translated and arranged by Isabel Florence Hapgood, fourth edition (Brooklyn: Syrian Antiochian Orthodox Archdiocese, 1965), p. 101.

3. Evelyn Underhill, *Worship* (New York: Harper & Row, 1937). See especially her description of God as presented in the Psalter, pp. 213-17. For a negative evaluation of Underhill, which he presents as an illustration of "the uncritical view of Christian worship," see Frederick Herzog, "The Norm and Freedom of Christian Worship," in *Worship in Scripture and Tradition*, edited by Massey H. Shepherd, Jr. (New York: Oxford University Press, 1963), pp. 98-133.

4. A very useful collection of these studies is found in *Understanding Church Growth and Decline 1950–1978*, edited by Dean R. Hoge and David A. Roozen (Philadelphia: Pilgrim Press, 1978). A related interpretation of these studies is Carl S. Dudley's *Where Have All Our People Gone?* (Philadelphia: Pilgrim Press, 1979).

5. Peter Jenkins, *A Walk Across America* (New York: Fawcett Crest Books, 1980). The first quotation is from pp. 153-54; and the second is from pp. 276, 287.

6. I have drawn heavily upon the recent publications of the liturgy committee of the Central Conference of American Rabbis. *Gates of Prayer: The New Union Prayerbook* (published by the Conference in 1975) gives services for weekdays, sabbaths, and festivals, as well as services and prayers for synagogue and home. *Gates of Repentance* (published in 1978) gives services and prayers for the days of awe. These books are rooted in Jewish tradition, yet deal also with contemporary experience and convictions. The editor and committee state that in this book the commitment in the Reform movement to the "equality of the sexes . . . takes the form of avoiding the use of masculine terminology exclusively when we are referring to the human race in general" (*Gates of Prayer*, p. xii). Chaim Stern served as editor for both books. *Gates of Understanding*, edited by Lawrence A. Hoffman, with notes by Chaim Stern and A. Stanley Dreyfus, and published in 1977 by the Union of American Hebrew Congregations for the Central Conference, contains interpretive essays and detailed notes on services in *Gates of Prayer*.

7. Joseph Heinemann, *Prayer in the Talmud: Forms and Patterns* (Berlin and New York: Walter de Gruyter, 1977). I have depended heavily upon Heinemann's analysis of Jewish prayers as they developed near the beginning of the Common Era. In his introduction Heinemann states: "We must also take into account the recorded opinions of the Mishnaic and Talmudic Sages on the subject of prayer—their attitudes, for example, toward the use of various divine epithets in prayer; their views on the role and the nature of praise in the worshipper's approach to God; their determination of the relative merits of individual as against communal prayer; their beliefs about the factors which may assist or prevent the acceptance of a petitioner's prayer; and so forth. We should, then, try to determine the extent to which these beliefs are reflected in the prayers themselves—in their style, structure, and content." His method is to apply "form-criticism to the field of Jewish liturgy" (p. 1). I have been directly influenced by his discussion of the liturgical *berakah*, pp. 82ff.

8. *Gates of Repentance*, pp. 260-61.

9. *Ibid.*, p. 87.

10. *Ibid.*, p. 100.

11. Theodore Parker, A *Discourse of Matters Pertaining to Religion*, fourth edition (Boston: Little, Brown, 1856), p. 152. The quotations from his prayers are taken from *Prayers*. A new edition with a preface by Louisa M. Alcott and a memoir by F. B. Sanborn (Boston: American Unitarian Association, 1901).

12. The groundbreaking study is Phyllis Trible's *God and the Rhetoric of Sexuality* (Philadelphia: Fortress Press, 1978), in which the author uses "a literary approach to hermeneutics" (p. 8). "To describe male and female," says Trible, "is to perceive the image of God; to perceive the image of God is to glimpse the transcendence of God" (p. 21). See also: Paul D. Hanson, "Masculine Metaphors for God and Sex-discrimination in the Old Testament," in *The Ecumenical Review* (see note 1, chapter 1); Virginia Ramey Mollenkott, *Women, Men, & the Bible* (Nashville: Abingdon, 1977); Letty M. Russell, ed., *The Liberating Word: A Guide to Non-Sexist Interpretation of the Bible* (Philadelphia: The Westminster Press, 1976).

13. Trible, *God and the Rhetoric of Sexuality*, p. 38.

14. Here I have adopted rhetorical terminology used by Trible. A metaphor, she says, moves from something that is "better known" to something that is lesser known. The better-known element is called the *vehicle* and is "the base of the metaphor," while "the tenor is its underlying (or overarching) subject, the lesser known element," p. 17.

15. Joseph Fort Newton, *Altar Stairs: A Little Book of Prayer* (New York: The Macmillan Co., 1928), p. 62.

16. *Gates of Prayer*, p. 287.

17. This quotation is from the liturgical Psalter published in *The Book of Common Prayer* (1977).

Chapter 4 Making Room

1. My efforts to test the use of these principles are illustrated in the latter portion of this book.

2. A brief discussion of the early history of Protestant church music is found in Horton Davies, *Worship and Theology in England; Vol. I, From Cranmer to Hooker, 1534–1603* (Princeton: Princeton University Press, 1970), pp. 377-404. See also Waldo Selden Pratt, *The Music of the French Psalter of 1562* (New York: A.M.S. Press, 1966; original issue, 1939); John Alexander Lamb, *The Psalms in Christian Worship* (London: Faith Press, 1962).

3. *Liturgy of the Hours* is a name now used for a structure of reading and praying often called the *Daily Office*. It began in the earliest days of the church's life and was developed more fully in the monastic communities later on. *The Liturgy of the Hours* provides a pattern of prayer for several times of the day and is built on the core of reciting the Psalms. *The Liturgy of the Hours* has been extensively revised since Vatican II, and the new form is discussed in *General Instruction on the Liturgy of the Hours*, translation and commentary by William A. Jurgens (Collegeville, Minn.: The Liturgical Press, 1975).

4. For a detailed and technical discussion of second- and third-person usage in Hebrew prayer, see Heinemann, *Prayer in the Talmud: Forms and Patterns*, pp. 77 ff.

5. *Lutheran Book of Worship: Minister's Desk Edition*, p. 15.

6. For a brief statement about amens at the end of hymns see Percy Dearmer, *Songs of Praise Discussed* (London: Oxford University Press, 1933), p. 375.

7. Erik Routley, "Sexist Language: A View from a Distance," *Worship* 53 (1979), pp. 2-11.

8. *Creation Sings*, edited by Ann Lodge (Philadelphia: The Geneva Press, 1980).

9. This procedure is used by James F. White in *Introduction to Christian Worship* (Nashville: Abingdon, 1980).

Chapter 5 Memory and Hope

1. A brief description of the new cult of the Goddess is Starhawk's "Witchcraft and Women's Culture," in *Womanspirit Rising* (see note 1, chapter 1), pp. 259-68.

2. Lectionaries can be described as "orderly sequences of selections from Scripture to be read aloud at public worship by a religious community." Currently the most widely used table of readings was developed by the Roman Catholic Church following Vatican II, and now adapted for use by major Protestant bodies in the United States. This lectionary presents three readings (ordinarily Old Testament, Epistle, and Gospel) for each Sunday and holy day for a three-year period. With slight variations this lectionary is used in the *Lutheran Book of Worship* and *The Book of Common Prayer*. It is also published in *A Lectionary* (Princeton: Consultation on Church Union), and the United Methodist Supplemental Worship Resources 6: *Seasons of the Gospel* (Nashville: Abingdon, 1979). An excellent group of evaluative essays is published in *Interpretation*

31, number 2 (April 1977). The above definition of lectionaries is from an essay in that journal, John Reumann's "A History of Lectionaries."

3. The current authority on the science of Bible translating is Eugene A. Nida, *Towards a Science of Translating* (Leiden: E. J. Brill, 1964). See also Harry Thomas and William L. Reed, eds., *Translating and Understanding the Old Testament* (Nashville: Abingdon, 1970); Frederick C. Grant, *Translating the Bible* (New York: The Seabury Press, 1961). An illuminating series of books is published for the United Bible Societies, under the title *A Translator's Handbook on*. . . . I am aware of volumes on *Paul's Letter to the Galatians* (1976), *Paul's Letter to the Philippians* (1977), *Paul's Letter to the Romans* (1973), *Paul's Letters to the Thessalonians* (1975), *The Acts of the Apostles* (1972), *The Book of Ruth* (1973), *The Gospel of Luke* (1971), *The Gospel of Mark* (1961), *The Letters of John* (1972).

4. The continuing "stand-by" is *Analytical Concordance to the Bible*, by Robert Young (Grand Rapids: Eerdmans Publishing Co., 1955).

5. Many people have a longer list. The United Methodist Section on Worship, for example, has decided that there are seven places in the liturgy which do not permit the ambiguity of titles such as "Almighty God" or "Eternal God." These places are: "at the beginning of the preface of the eucharistic prayer, in the doxology at its conclusion, the parallel doxology at the end of the prayer over the water in the baptismal rite, in the baptismal formula itself, in the Lord's Prayer, in the Apostles' Creed and in the Nicene Creed. In these instances, there was need to be specific for both theological and ecumenical reasons." James F. White, "Justice and the Work of Liturgical Renewal." *Christianity and Crisis*, Vol. 40, No. 10 (June 9, 1980), p. 174.

6. The best-known point of view about Jesus' use of the title Father is that of J. Jeremias, which is presented in his *The Lord's Prayer*, translated by John Reumann (Philadelphia: Fortress Press, 1964). Jeremias stresses the uniqueness of Jesus' use of the title *Abba*, which he interprets as "the address of the small child to his father" (p. 19). This childlike relation is here seen as "the heart of the revelation" granted to Jesus (p. 20). A more balanced point of view characterizes the essays in *The Lord's Prayer and Jewish Liturgy*, edited by Jakob J. Petuchowski and Michael Brocke (New York: The Seabury Press, 1978). John M. Oesterreicher declares that Jeremias is "misleading." Oesterreicher's view is that Jesus drew upon a strong Jewish tradition but that he stamped it with "his personal impress." (See Oesterreicher's essay, "'Abba, Father!' On the Humanity of Jesus," pp. 119-36.)

The title Father does convey a strong sense of God's identification with Jesus in his suffering. As Oesterreicher states it "the almighty God is at the same time the all-merciful." He suggests that Jesus' experience of God includes both the intimacy Jeremias accents and the sense of God's power. His address in Gethsemane could be translated "*Abba*, You all-powerful One" (p. 125).

It is at this point that we can understand the most powerful argument against calling God Father, an argument far more substantial than those based on culturally conditioned sexist bias. How can God be silent in the face of modern terror, which reached its culmination in the holocaust? If one of the claims of fatherhood is to accept a certain responsibility for everything that his children do, then how can God be excused from implication in the crimes the Nazis inflicted upon Jews and others? See the essay by Walter Strolz, "The Fatherhood of God in Modern Interpretations," pp. 191-203.

7. "An Affirmation of the Baptismal Covenant," published by the Commission on Worship of the Consultation on Church Union (Princeton, 1980), pp. 4, 10.

Chapter 6 The Dynamics of Change

1. *Book of Prayer for Personal Use,* fourth edition (Collegeville, Minn.: Saint John's Abbey Press, 1975), pp. 8, 12. Monday of Week 11 appears on pp. 436-37.

2. Frances E. Willard, *A Wheel Within a Wheel* (Chicago: Women's Temperance Publishing Association, 1895), p. 10.

3. I have been influenced by the argument given by Clement Welsh, *Preaching in a New Key* (Philadelphia: Pilgrim Press, 1974), especially pp. 71-117.

4. The chief liturgical officers in the Christian Church (Disciples of Christ) and related church bodies are elders and deacons, elected from the membership of the congregation, and the pastor. It is the normal practice for two elders to offer the Communion prayers every Sunday during the celebration of the Lord's Supper (which is conducted weekly in these congregations). Pastors ordinarily introduce the service and recite the words of institution. Deacons distribute the bread and cup to the congregation. For fuller discussion see my "Worship in the Christian Church (Disciples of Christ)," *Worship* 51 (1977), 486-96; "Ministers and Elders as Leaders of Worship in the Christian Church (Disciples of Christ)," *Encounter* 39 (1978), 305-32; *The Feast of Joy* (St. Louis: Bethany Press, 1977).

5. Much of the current literature has been generated by debates concerning ordaining women in the Roman Catholic and Episcopal Churches. A sampling of this literature includes; Haye van der Meer, S.J., *Women Priests in the Catholic Church?* translated by Arlene and Leonard Swidler (Philadelphia: Temple University Press, 1973); *Women Priests: A Catholic Commentary on the Vatican Declaration,* edited by Leonard Swidler and Arlene Swidler (Paramus, N.J.: Paulist/Newman Press, 1977); James A. Coriden, *Sexism and Church Law* (Paramus, N.J.: Paulist/Newman Press, 1977); *Women Priests: Yes or No?* by Emily C. Hewitt and Suzanne R. Hiatt (New York: The Seabury Press, 1973).

Chapter 7 But Are the People Ready?

1. This service by Ricciuti, with introduction, is included in *Sistercelebrations: Nine Worship Experiences* (see note 1, chapter 1), pp. 1-8.

2. Ellen and Dana Cherry, "Brit Kedusha: A Home Ceremony Celebrating the Birth of a Daughter," *Sistercelebrations,* pp. 20-26.

3. H. Grady Davis, *Design for Preaching* (Philadelphia: Fortress Press, 1958), pp. 154-55.

4. Spiritual direction is increasingly important as a part of pastoral work. Among the useful writings on this discipline are: *Soul Friend,* by Kenneth Leach (London: Sheldon Press, 1977); *Spiritual Friend: Reclaiming the Gift of Spiritual Direction,* by Tilden H. Edwards (Paramus, N.J.: Paulist/Newman Press, 1980); "Contemporary Spiritual Direction: Scope and Principle," by William J. Connolly, S.J. (*Studies in the Spirituality of Jesuits,* vol. 7).

Chapter 9 Workbook for the Lord's Day Service

1. I have consulted Artur Weiser's *The Psalms: A Commentary* (Philadelphia: The Westminster Press, 1962) in preparing all the comments on these psalms.

2. *Ibid.,* p. 202.